D0297044

GI high-energy cookbook

RYLAND
PETERS
& SMALL

LONDON NEW YORK

GI high-energy cookbook

low-GI recipes for weight loss, health and vitality

rachael anne hill *photography by nicky dowey*

Editor Sharon Ashman
Production Deborah Wehner
Art Director Gabriella Le Grazie
Publishing Director Alison Starling

Recipe Tester Gina Steer
Food Stylist Lucy McKelvie
Stylist Liz Belton
Indexer Hilary Bird

First published in Great Britain in 2004
by Ryland Peters & Small
20–21 Jockey's Fields
London WC1R 4BW
www.rylandpeters.com

10 9 8 7 6 5 4

Text © Rachael Anne Hill 2004
Design and photographs
© Ryland Peters & Small 2004

The author's moral rights have been
asserted. All rights reserved. No part
of this publication may be reproduced,
stored in a retrieval system or
transmitted in any form or by any means,
electronic, mechanical, photocopying
or otherwise, without the prior
permission of the publisher.

ISBN 1 84172 571 4

A catalogue record for this book
is available from the British Library.

Printed in China

Notes

All spoon measurements are level unless otherwise stated.

Ovens should be preheated to the specified temperature.
If using a fan-assisted oven, cooking times should be reduced
according to the manufacturer's instructions.

Uncooked or partly cooked eggs should not be served to the
very young, the very old or frail, or to pregnant women.

All fruits and vegetables should be washed thoroughly and
peeled, unless otherwise stated. Unwaxed citrus fruits should
be used whenever possible.

Every effort has been made by the author and the publisher to
ensure that the information given in this book is complete and
accurate. This book is not intended as a substitute for proper
medical advice. Always consult your doctor on matters regarding
health. Neither the author nor the publisher shall be held
responsible for any loss, injury or damage allegedly arising from
any information or suggestion in this book.

contents

the glycaemic index explained

What's the problem?

Do you suffer from any of the following:

excess weight

general tiredness, particularly mid-afternoon

flagging energy levels that can be boosted by eating something

lack of concentration

tiredness or grogginess even after a good night's sleep

mood swings

food cravings, especially for sweet, fatty foods mid-afternoon or after eating a meal

high blood pressure

high cholesterol

craving for alcohol early in the evening

diabetes

heart disease

The chances are that you do suffer from one or more of these symptoms. In fact, tiredness is the most common complaint cited in doctors' surgeries today. A shocking 50 per cent of all UK adults are overweight and the number of seriously obese adults has trebled in the last 20 years. The amount of adults diagnosed with diabetes has doubled in the past 20 years and those developing heart disease has increased by 25 per cent since the late 1980s, resulting in 2.65 million people now living with this crippling condition. These are frightening statistics but perhaps even more frightening is the fact that we are not alone. Take a close look at almost any Western country and you will find a similar picture emerging.

Where are we going wrong?

The real key to understanding why so many of us are experiencing such health problems lies in our past. The diet and lifestyle of Westerners have changed almost beyond recognition over the past century. This in itself wouldn't be a problem if it wasn't for the fact that our basic physiology and biochemistry remain almost exactly the same as those of our ancestors 1,000 years ago. Consequently, there is a mismatch between the foods that we eat and the foods that our bodies really need.

Although our ancestors ate the same amount of calories as we do today, if not more, they were much more active than we are and obtained considerably fewer of their calories from carbohydrates. The carbohydrates they did eat came in the form of beans, vegetables, wholegrain cereals, fibrous fruits and berries. Lack of refrigeration and little knowledge of food processing meant that much of this food remained relatively unchanged from the field to the plate. Consequently, most of the processing of their food was done by the body after they had eaten it. This took the body a long time, resulting in a gradual, sustained release of sugars into the bloodstream, leaving them feeling full and satisfied for longer.

By contrast, today flour is ground as thin as talcum powder to enable us to bake the lightest, fluffiest cakes and breads. Preferred fruit varieties are those that are high in sugar and low in fibre because they taste better. Cereals are so highly processed that they become unrecognizable, then refined sugars are added to them to make many of the foods we see on our supermarket shelves. Fibre-filled pulses are often absent from our food cupboards. Instead they have been replaced by highly refined, fatty, 'fast' foods that take little time to prepare and even less time to digest.

As a result, almost every meal we eat contains the sorts of carbohydrates that break down quickly and release their sugars rapidly into the bloodstream, such as baked potatoes, chips, easy-cook rice, biscuits, cereals, cakes, breads and fast foods. And it is these foods that are contributing to many of our health problems. While it may not be possible or even desirable to return to eating habits of old, thanks to extensive testing of carbohydrate foods by leading researchers, we can now monitor the sorts of carbs we eat by referring to something called the 'glycaemic index'.

What is the glycaemic index?

The glycaemic index (GI) is a scientific ranking of foods based on their immediate effect on blood sugar levels. Many everyday carbohydrate-based foods have been tested and given a ranking between 1 and 100, depending on the speed at which they release their sugars into the bloodstream (see page 21). Carbohydrate foods that break down quickly during digestion have the highest glycaemic indices (GIs of 70 or above). Their blood sugar response is fast and high. Carbohydrates that break down slowly, releasing glucose gradually into the bloodstream, have low glycaemic indices (GIs of less than 55).

Up until recently, it was believed that carbohydrates could be divided into two main categories – 'simple' and 'complex'. Simple carbohydrates consisted of sweet, sugary foods, such as cakes, biscuits, sweets, chocolate, jam and honey. Complex carbohydrates consisted of the more starchy foods, such as bread, potatoes, rice, pasta and cereals. It was commonly thought that the sweet, simple carbohydrates caused our blood sugar levels to rise far more rapidly and give us a quicker energy burst than the starchy, complex ones. Now however, thanks to the creation of the glycaemic index, we know this not to be the case and foods such as baked potatoes and some types of bread tend to have a far higher GI and cause a far greater surge in blood sugar levels than many sweeter, more sugary foods.

EXAMPLES OF HIGH-GI FOODS	
FOOD	**GI RATING**
Baguette	95
Baked potato	85
Rice cakes	85
Cornflakes	84
Puffed rice cereal	82
Puffed crispbread	81
Water biscuits	78
Chips	75
Tortilla/corn chips	72
White bread	70
Mashed potato	70

EXAMPLES OF LOW-GI FOODS	
FOOD	**GI RATING**
Apple	36
Yoghurt (low fat)	33
Skimmed milk	32
Dried apricots	31
Canned peaches (in juice)	30
Red kidney beans	27
Red lentils	26
Grapefruit	25
Cherries	22
Soya beans	18
Peanuts	14

What's the problem with eating high-GI foods?

The sugars in high-GI foods are broken down quickly so they do not supply a sustained source of energy. Instead, they cause our blood sugar levels to rise rapidly. The body has to respond to this by making large quantities of the blood sugar-lowering hormone, insulin, and releasing it into the blood. Unfortunately, insulin is often too good at its job and instead of just reducing blood sugar levels to a desirable level, it sends them plummeting to levels lower than they were originally. This sets up a yo-yo effect as the body then responds by making us crave fatty, sugary foods in an attempt to make our blood sugar levels rise once more. Many of the symptoms listed on page 8 can be linked to fluctuating blood sugar levels caused by eating too many carbohydrate foods that score high on the glycaemic index.

Food cravings and lethargy

Many of us experience this yo-yo effect as the 'mid-afternoon lull'. We eat a high-GI lunch – sandwiches or a baked potato, for example – and by 3.30pm we are not only feeling tired, lethargic and lacking in concentration, but we are positively craving something sweet to give us that much needed energy boost. This often happens again after the evening meal when we find ourselves heading back to the kitchen for a dessert, some chocolate biscuits or a glass of wine just a short while after having eaten.

Weight gain

A diet rich in high-GI foods can cause you to eat more calories (and therefore gain weight) for two reasons. The first is that high-GI foods are quick to break down. The quicker a food breaks down, the sooner you will become hungry and the more likely you will be to want to eat again. Secondly, high-GI foods will cause your blood sugar levels to rapidly rise and then fall, which in turn will result in strong urges to eat fatty, sugary foods shortly after a meal. Both points

are compounded by the fact that another of insulin's main roles is to promote fat storage, so the more insulin you have in your blood the more likely you are to store any excess calories you eat as fat.

Lack of concentration and mood swings

The brain is entirely fuelled by blood sugar. Therefore when levels drop as a result of the excessive production of insulin, it becomes more difficult to concentrate. Research has also found that low blood sugar levels are often linked to mood swings, reduced reaction times and even depression.

Diabetes

Diabetes is one of the most common health problems in the world, but it is most prevalent in Western cultures where we tend to eat a diet rich in highly

---

A WORD ABOUT WEIGHT LOSS

The average woman needs about 2,000 calories per day to maintain her current weight; the average man needs about 2,500. However, if you want to lose weight it is advisable to reduce your calorie intake by 500–600 calories per day, but no more. If your calorie intake drops too low – to less than 1,200 per day – you will simply encourage your body to become better at storing fat. So although you may lose weight initially, in the longer term you will put it all back on and more besides!

processed, refined foods. It is thought that the stress that high-GI foods place on the body to keep blood sugar levels constant can result in either the insulin not working properly or the pancreas, the manufacturing site of insulin, becoming less efficient at producing it, sometimes giving up altogether.

Heart disease

As we have already seen, a diet rich in high-GI foods can result in people becoming overweight or developing diabetes. Obesity and diabetes are two of the principal risk factors that can lead to heart disease. In addition, high levels of insulin, which are brought about as a result of eating high-GI foods, are strongly linked to increased blood pressure and cholesterol (along with other blood fats), both of which are also major contributing factors to heart disease.

What are the benefits of a low-GI diet?

There are many health reasons for switching to a low-GI diet. It will not only help you to lose weight (if you have excess weight to lose) but research has shown that a diet rich in low-GI foods can reduce your risk of getting heart disease, diabetes and cancer by as much as 50 per cent. This is due to their ability to promote weight loss, lower blood pressure and cholesterol levels and boost the body's ability to fight disease by strengthening the immune system.

REASONS FOR SWITCHING TO A LOW-GI DIET

A low-GI diet is:

Naturally more filling so you will automatically take in fewer calories

Higher in fibre, which can help to reduce your cholesterol levels

More sustaining, giving far greater energy levels throughout the day

Higher in essential vitamins, minerals and antioxidants, which help to keep your immune system strong and healthy

Higher in fruit and vegetable content. Research shows that a diet rich in fruits and vegetables can reduce the risk of developing certain cancers by up to 40 per cent

---

How do I switch to a healthy, low-GI diet?

If you follow the guidelines below you will automatically cut back on energy-draining, high-GI foods, such as refined breads, cakes and biscuits. You will also consume less fat, particularly saturated fat, and fewer calories. These changes in your diet will help to keep you feeling full and energized and, combined with regular exercise and an active lifestyle, any excess pounds you are carrying will begin to disappear – for good.

Base your meals around low-GI foods but remember to choose foods that are also low in saturated fat

Saturated fat increases the likelihood of developing heart disease by clogging the arteries and increasing cholesterol levels. It can also make you less responsive to insulin, which means your body needs to make more of it, possibly boosting appetite and weight as a result.

Eat seven or more servings of fruits and vegetables every day

There is overwhelming research to prove that a diet high in fruits and vegetables will significantly help to reduce your risk of developing many cancers and other life-threatening diseases. They also help with weight loss because they are low in calories and fat. Aim to eat at least three or four servings of vegetables a day and two or three servings of fruit. Eat as wide a variety of different fruits and vegetables as possible, and as many different coloured ones as you can to ensure you are getting plenty of immune-boosting antioxidants, which help fight disease.

WHY DON'T FOODS LIKE MEAT, FISH, CHICKEN AND AVOCADOS APPEAR ON THE GLYCAEMIC INDEX?

The glycaemic index is a measure of how quickly the carbohydrate within a food is broken down and released into the blood. Foods such as meat, fish, chicken and avocados contain no or very little carbohydrate, therefore they do not need to be tested. This is also true of many fruits and vegetables.

Eat at least two low-GI meals a day

Ideally every meal we eat would be low GI, but busy lifestyles and the availability of fast foods means this doesn't always happen. However, the good news is that the effect of a low-GI meal carries over to the subsequent meal, reducing its glycaemic impact. Therefore, even if just two of your meals a day are low GI, the chances are you will retain fairly even blood sugar levels.

Eat wholegrain breads and cereals with a low GI

Not only are wholegrain foods slower releasing and therefore more sustaining for longer, but they will also increase your fibre intake which in turn will help to reduce your cholesterol level and your waistline. Research also shows that an increased consumption of wholegrains is associated with a significantly reduced incidence of cancer and heart disease. One study of over 34,000 women found that the risk of death from ischemic heart disease was reduced by 33 per cent in those that ate one or more servings of wholegrain foods per day.

Eat more pulses

Base meals around beans, peas and lentils instead of potatoes and high-GI rice (like the easy-cook variety). Pulses are slow releasing and nutrient dense, providing protein, fibre, iron, calcium, folate and soluble fibre (the type that really helps to lower cholesterol levels). They are also an excellent source of phytoestrogens, which can help to reduce the risk of many lifestyle diseases, including certain cancers, can help to control menopausal symptoms and increase the immune system's ability to fight infections.

Eat more nuts and seeds

It is often assumed, especially by people looking to lose weight, that because nuts are high in fat they should be avoided. However, this is not the case. Nuts are not only very low GI and therefore very filling, but many of them are also great sources of essential fatty acids. Essential fatty acids are the only fats that cannot be manufactured by the body and therefore have to come exclusively from our diet. Evidence is amassing that an adequate intake of essential fatty acids may help to prevent or control all kinds of ailments, including heart disease, cancer, immune system deficiencies, arthritis, skin complaints, premenstrual syndrome and menopausal symptoms.

Eat oily fish or seafood two or three times a week

Oily fish, such as mackerel, sardines, herring, trout, fresh (not canned) tuna and salmon, and other types of seafood are excellent sources of essential fatty acids, in particular omega-3. Just one serving of oily fish a week can reduce the tendency of the blood to clot, and therefore lower the likelihood of suffering a fatal heart attack, by as much as 40 per cent. However, it is not advisable to eat oily fish more than three times a week as it can lead to a high intake of dioxins due to pollution from the sea. Also, farmed fish appear to have a lower concentration of omega-3 fatty acids than wild fish, so go for wild fish whenever possible.

THE IMPORTANCE OF EXERCISE

Research shows that activity and exercise increase the efficiency of insulin in the body and therefore lower the risk of experiencing many of the health problems associated with a high-GI diet.

Eat lean meats at least two or three times a week

Meat is a great source of iron. Instead of cutting it out of your diet as many people trying to reduce their saturated fat intake tend to do, choose lean meat and chicken instead. Cut away any visible fat and use cooking methods such as grilling or barbecuing to help keep the fat content even lower.

Choose low-fat dairy products

Dairy foods are great sources of bone-strengthening calcium, so make sure you eat two or three servings a day in the form of skimmed milk, low-fat yoghurt and low-fat cheese or cottage cheese.

Replace sugary drinks with fresh fruit juices, skimmed milk and water

Sugary drinks, especially sports drinks, can have a GI rating as high as 95 and often contain a lot of empty calories, so it's best to avoid them. Try to limit tea and coffee to two or three cups a day, too. Research shows that caffeine can block the absorption of vitamins and minerals while sugar, with a GI rating of 65, in tea and coffee will also significantly raise your blood sugar levels. Fresh, unsweetened fruit juices, skimmed milk and water are far better alternatives as they score much lower on the glycaemic index. Fruit juices also contain the added bonus of extra vitamins and minerals, while skimmed milk is a good source of calcium.

THE GI CHART SHOWS THAT SOME FRUITS AND VEGETABLES HAVE A HIGH-GI VALUE. DOES THIS MEAN THAT I SHOULD AVOID THEM?

No. You can eat most fruits and vegetables without even considering their GI value. This is because even those with a high GI value won't usually contain enough carbohydrate to have a significant effect on your blood sugar levels.

WOULDN'T IT BE SIMPLER TO JUST CUT OUT CARBOHYDRATE-BASED FOODS ALTOGETHER?

No. High-protein, low-carbohydrate diets have become very popular again over recent years since many people have been led to believe that carbohydrates are bad for you and cause excess weight to be gained. This is not the case. In fact, carbohydrates are very important in the diet for a number of reasons:

1) Carbohydrates are broken down to form glucose and glycogen and fat can only be burnt and used as energy if carbohydrate (glucose) is present. If we don't eat enough carbohydrate our body responds by breaking down our lean muscle tissue and turning it into glucose. This is something we should avoid at all costs because a loss of lean muscle tissue automatically causes a decline in our metabolic rate which in turn causes us to gain more fat.

2) The brain can only function if carbohydrate (glucose) is present.

3) Carbohydrate is broken down and stored as glycogen in our muscles to give us energy. If we don't eat enough carbohydrate our glycogen stores become depleted leaving us feeling tired, shaky and often experiencing headaches.

4) Carbohydrate foods are natural appetite suppressors.

5) Carbohydrate is less likely to be stored as fat on the body. For every 100 kcals of carbohydrate we overeat, only 75 will be stored as fat. This is because the body uses 25 of those calories turning the carbohydrate into fat. However, for every 100 kcals of fat we overeat, our body only uses 2 kcals of energy to store it.

Eat small, regular meals

Research shows that even low-GI foods can cause blood sugar levels to soar when eaten in large quantities. It is therefore better to graze throughout the day on small meals and healthy, low-fat, low-GI snacks than to eat three large meals a day.

Eat a wide variety of foods

A food is not good or bad based solely on its GI value. Just because a food has a high GI rating, it shouldn't be excluded from the diet. Simply eat it in smaller quantities and try to reduce its effect on blood sugar levels by combining it with a low-GI food or a high-protein food, such as lean meat, fish or chicken. Studies show that when a high-GI food is eaten with a low-GI or high-protein food, the effect of the high-GI food on blood sugar levels is reduced.

Prepare and cook as much of your own food as you can

There is a common misconception that cooking meals from scratch is difficult and/or time consuming. A myth that is probably perpetuated by the vast numbers of supermarkets, fast food companies, restaurants and takeaways that have a vested interest in keeping us out of the kitchen. In reality, as you'll see from the recipes in this book, it takes very little time or effort to put together really healthy, low-fat, delicious meals. The benefit of preparing meals yourself is that not only are they likely to be much fresher and therefore higher in vitamins and minerals than pre-prepared shop-bought alternatives, you can also exercise far greater control over what you are actually putting into your body. Shop-bought meals and snacks are likely to be much higher in fats, sugars, additives and preservatives and therefore worse for you than anything you make for yourself. So don't be overwhelmed, step back into the kitchen and try out some of these simple recipes. You'll be amazed at just how quick, easy and delicious low-GI eating can be!

---

5 WAYS TO LOWER THE GI OF YOUR MEALS

1) Mix high-GI foods with low-GI foods – research shows that a high-GI food combined with a low-GI food of the same carbohydrate quantity will result in an intermediate GI for the overall meal.

2) Eat protein with your carbohydrates – high-protein foods, such as lean meat, chicken and fish, tend to slow the rate at which a meal is digested and therefore lower the GI of the overall meal.

3) Choose vegetables first – all too often we base our meals around the carbohydrate-rich food, such as pasta, potatoes or rice. Instead, first plan your meal around the vegetables you hope to use, then around the protein-rich foods, such as meat, fish or pulses, and then the carbohydrate-rich food. This will automatically help to lower the GI of a meal.

4) Use beans and pulses as often as possible – try puréeing them to make sauces, cooking them in stews, serving them with fresh herbs as side dishes, adding them to salads, making them into dips or using mashed beans or lentils instead of mashed potatoes.

5) Keep cooking times to a minimum – cooked foods often have a higher GI than uncooked foods, so make sure your pasta is *al dente* and your vegetables are cooked for the shortest time possible. This will also help to retain more of their vitamins and minerals.

Putting a low-GI diet into practice

BREAKFAST

Eat more

Fresh fruits – particularly apples, pears, plums, cherries, peaches, berries and citrus fruits

Low-fat dairy products, such as skimmed milk and low-fat yoghurts

Low-GI cereals, such as oats, muesli, bran sticks and oat or rice bran

Low GI breads, such as wholegrain, nutty varieties and rye bread. Don't be fooled by thinking that just because a bread is wholemeal it is low GI. Plain, wholemeal bread has almost the same GI rating (69) as white bread (70) so make sure you go for breads that contain wholegrains, nuts and seeds

Oily fish, such as mackerel, salmon and kippers (see page 34)

Lean red meat, such as extra lean bacon and ham (see page 33)

Nuts and seeds – sprinkled on cereals, fruit salads and yoghurts and baked in breads and muffins (see page 25).

Unsweetened, fresh fruit juices

Vegetable juices

Fruit-based smoothies (page 39)

Eat less

Sugar in tea and on cereals

Refined, processed breakfast cereals

White and wholemeal breads, croissants and bagels

High-fat, high-sugar pastries

High-sugar jams, marmalades and spreads

Fatty meats, such as bacon and sausages

Full-fat dairy products, such as milk, yoghurts and cheeses

Sweetened, processed fruit juices

LUNCH

Eat more

Open sandwiches on rye or wholegrain bread (see page 42)

Wholemeal pita breads (see page 44)

Baked sweet potatoes (see page 73)

Cracked wheat, pasta and noodles

Baked beans

Vegetable soups with pulses or barley (see page 64)

Salads made with beans, nuts and pulses (see pages 46, 47 and 48)

Fresh fruit

Naturally low-fat cheeses, such as ricotta, Edam or cottage cheese or low-fat varieties of feta and Cheddar cheese

Lean meat, fish and chicken

Raw vegetables such as grated carrot in a salad or sticks of celery and florets of broccoli and cauliflower used as crudités

Salad dressings made from lemon juice and vinegars

Eat less

Traditional sandwiches

Baked potatoes

Crisps

Sugary snacks

White and wholemeal breads, croissants and bagels

High-fat, high-sugar pastries

Mayonnaise and high-fat dressings

High-fat cheeses, such as Brie, Stilton and cream cheese

Full-fat yoghurts and desserts

SNACKS

Eat more

Oat-based snacks, such as low-fat flapjack (page 56) or yoghurt topped with muesli

Fresh fruit, such as grapes, diced pineapple, puréed mango and banana in a smoothie, or freshly sliced kiwi fruit

Nuts and seeds

Fruit cake (see page 61)

Oatmeal biscuits (see page 57) and muffins (see page 25)

Low-fat yoghurts

Dried fruit

Lentil spreads (see page 45) and hoummus (see page 99) with vegetable crudités, such as celery and carrot sticks and broccoli and cauliflower florets

Wholegrain and rye breads

Good-quality chocolate (70 per cent cocoa content or above)

Eat Less

Low-cocoa chocolate and other sweets

Crisps

Salted, roasted peanuts

Pastries and cakes

EVENING MEALS

Eat more

Home-prepared meals

Vegetables in soups, stews, casseroles, stir fries, salads, curries and rice dishes

Salads either as a starter, side dish or a main meal

Beans and pulses as side dishes or the basis of a meal (see pages 74 and 81)

Lean meat, chicken and fish

Noodles, pasta, and low-GI rice, such as basmati

Sweet potatoes and yams

Eat less

Potato-based meals, such as chips, mashed or baked potatoes

Refined breads and pizza bases

Ready-prepared meals

Take-out meals

Easy-cook and white rice (other than basmati)

Quantity by keeping meals small. Even low-GI foods eaten in large quantities can cause blood sugar levels to rise suddenly.

PUDDINGS

Eat more

Fruit-based desserts (see pages 116 and 122)

Low-fat crème fraîche and yoghurt

Eat less

Cream and full-fat yoghurts

Desserts made with refined sugar

CAN I EAT AS MUCH LOW-GI FOOD AS I LIKE?

No. Just because a food is low GI doesn't give it the green light to be eaten in large quantities. It can still lead to weight gain, especially if it is high in fat and calories. That's why the three main factors to consider when choosing which foods should make up the majority of your diet are:

1) The GI rating of the food

2) The fat content of the food

3) The amount of the food that you are eating – even low-GI foods, such as pasta, can stimulate big releases of insulin if eaten in large quantities. So keep portions small but eat at frequent intervals throughout the day.

Shopping tips

This is the essential low-GI, high-energy shopping list. It contains pretty much everything you will need to make all the recipes in this book. However, it also doubles as a great shopping guide for anyone wishing to adopt a low-GI diet.

Bread

100 per cent wholewheat, nutty, grainy breads

Tortillas

Wholemeal pita bread

Linseed rye bread

Pasta, rice and noodles

Fettuccine

Vermicelli

Linguine

Macaroni

Wholewheat spaghetti

Basmati rice

Rice noodles

Egg noodles

Cereals and grains

Jumbo oats

Bran sticks

Bulgur wheat

Pearl barley

Beans and pulses

Canned beans, including red kidney, cannellini, butter, mixed, haricot, aduki, borlotti, pinto, baked beans and refried beans

Canned chickpeas

Red and green split lentils

Baking and cooking

Wholemeal flour

Oatmeal

Baking powder

Cornflour

Mixed spice

Ground cinnamon

Cinnamon sticks

Five spice powder

Wheat/oat bran

Dried, ready-to-eat apricots

Sultanas

Nuts and seeds

Peanuts

Flaked almonds

Walnuts

Brazil nuts

Hazelnuts

Sunflower seeds

Sesame seeds

Linseeds

Dairy

Skimmed milk

Low-fat crème fraîche

Low-fat fromage frais

Low-fat vanilla ice cream or frozen yoghurt

Low-fat (preferably sugar-free or reduced-sugar) natural and fruit yoghurts

Low-fat cottage cheese

Reduced-fat Cheddar and feta cheese

Parmesan cheese

Meat, poultry, fish and eggs

Extra-lean ham, bacon and minced beef

Parma ham

Turkey slices

Chicken breasts (skin removed)

Eggs

Mackerel (canned in brine and fresh)

Smoked salmon

Salmon fillets

Fresh tuna

Canned tuna

Cod

Haddock

King prawns

Scallops

Canned anchovies

Fruit

Any. Particularly fresh apples, pears, plums, cherries, peaches, strawberries, raspberries, blackberries, kiwi fruit, oranges, limes, lemons, grapefruit, red grapes

Canned fruit in fruit juice rather than syrup

Frozen mixed berries

Vegetables

Any! Just go easy on the potatoes—try sweet potatoes or small, new ones instead. Buy as many different coloured vegetables as possible to make sure you are getting plenty of immune-boosting antioxidants. Stock your freezer with frozen vegetables, too – they can be just as nutritious as fresh ones

Fats and oils

Olive oil, sunflower oil and sesame oil

Low-fat polyunsaturated spread

Storecupboard items

Vegetable and beef stock cubes

Fresh garlic

Fresh chillies

Fresh ginger

Lemongrass

Soy sauce

Worcestershire sauce

Tomato purée

Wholegrain mustard

Olives

Balsamic vinegar

Red wine vinegar

Sweet chilli sauce

Lemon juice

Good-quality dark chocolate (70 per cent plus cocoa solids)

Cranberry sauce

Peanut butter

Honey

Curry powder (medium)

Ground cumin

Chilli powder

Relish

Canned tomatoes

Capers

Canned artichoke hearts

Herbs

A selection of fresh herbs, such as coriander, basil, oregano, rosemary, chives, tarragon, parsley, sage and mint

Drinks

Unsweetened, fresh fruit and vegetable juices (preferably with pulp)

Eating out tips

Although it can be more difficult to maintain a low-GI diet when eating out, it certainly isn't impossible and it needn't be complicated. Don't be intimidated by a new menu, simply bear in mind that you have two main aims – to keep both the GI rating and the fat content (particularly the saturated fat content) of your meal as low as possible. Rest assured that you can achieve these aims no matter where you are by applying a few simple guidelines.

1. Keep the GI of a meal low

Avoid or only eat small amounts of:

High-GI foods, such as most forms of potato, including mashed, chipped and baked, most forms of rice (other than basmati), most breads and other highly refined carbohydrate-based foods, including sugary drinks and desserts

Go for:

Vegetables either in the form of a vegetable-based main course or order some extra vegetable side dishes to replace the chips, rice or potatoes that you might ordinarily have ordered

Salads, either as a main course, as a starter or as a side dish

Protein-based foods, such as lean meat, fish, chicken and pulses. The protein in these foods will help to significantly lower the GI rating of your overall meal

Fruit-based desserts instead of those laden with refined flour and sugar, and fat

2. Keep the saturated fat content low

Following the guidelines given on the left will not only help to lower the GI of your meal, they will also go a long way towards keeping the fat content of your meal low, too. However, in order to keep the saturated fat content of your meal low, do the following:

Avoid or only eat small amounts of:

Fried and roasted foods

High-fat foods, such as mayonnaise, butter and butter-based sauces, cheese, cream and fatty meats

Go for:

Oily fish and avocados – although the fat content and therefore the calorie content of these foods is high, they are packed full of good, healthy essential fatty acids

Specific Restaurants

Whatever type of restaurant you are in, just apply the two rules given on the left. However, the following information will help you make your menu choice in specialized restaurants.

Indian

Go for:

Tomato- or vegetable-based curries

Tandoori-style meat – marinated in yoghurt and spices and then cooked in a clay oven

Tikkas are lower in calories than many other curries because they are dry-roasted in a clay oven, but watch out for the high-fat sauces often served with them

Side salads and vegetable side dishes

Dishes based around lentils, pulses and vegetables, such as dhansak and dhal

Avoid or only eat small amounts of:

Creamy curries such as kormas or massalas

Rice, especially fried. If you must have rice ask for boiled basmati

Poppadoms and breads, such as naan, chapatti or paratha

Fried foods, such as onion bhajis and fried meats

Chinese and Thai

Go for:

Clear soups

Main courses based around vegetables or lean proteins, such as fish, pork or chicken

Noodle-based dishes, such as chow mein, but avoid fried noodles wherever possible

Thai salads

Steamed and stir-fried dishes

Avoid or only eat small amounts of:

Deep-fried foods, such as crispy seaweed, prawn toast and prawn crackers or those served in batter. They are usually high GI and high in fat

Rice-based dishes

Duck – it is very high in fat

Meals containing coconut or coconut milk or cream. These are particularly high in saturated fat

Mexican

Go for:

Salsa and tomato-based sauces

Tortillas filled with GI-lowering protein foods, such as grilled chicken and refried beans

Peppers

Salads

Guacamole – small amounts are great but don't overdo it, especially if you are trying to maintain or lose weight

Avoid or only eat small amounts of:

Sour cream

Cheese

Burgers

Nachos

Italian

Go for:

Salads, but use balsamic vinegar and small amounts of olive oil to dress your salad instead of high-fat alternatives, such as blue cheese or seafood mayonnaise

Tomato-based sauces, such as arrabbiata or neopolitan, instead of cream- or cheese-based sauces, such as carbonara

Olives

Spinach leaves either in salads or on pizzas

Lean grilled meats, such as ham and chicken

Fish, especially fresh tuna, which is high in essential omega-3 fatty acids

Pasta – the lowest-GI pastas are fettuccine, spaghetti, vermicelli, linguine and macaroni

Avoid or only eat small amounts of:

Breads, such as garlic bread, dough balls, bread sticks and pizza bases (choose thin bases rather than thick ones and load them with tomatoes and vegetables rather than cheese and fatty meats, such as salami or bacon)

Cream in sauces like carbonara or in coffees and puddings

Cheese in sauces, such as pesto or piled on top of pizzas

Too much oil. Although olive oil has many health-giving properties it is still possible to overdo it and consume too many calories

The GI ratings of some popular foods

Low-GI foods (below 55)   Medium-GI foods (55–70)   High-GI foods (above 70)

FRUIT AND VEGETABLES

Although some fruits and vegetables seem to score high on the glycaemic index, in reality when eaten in normal or even large quantities they contain such small amounts of carbohydrate that they have little or no measurable effect on blood sugar levels. Therefore, they should be eaten freely as the nutrients they contain do provide immense health benefits.

Fruit

Cherries	22
Grapefruit	25
Peach (canned in juice)	30
Apricot (dried)	31
Apple	38
Pear	38
Plum	39
Strawberries	40
Peach	42
Orange	44
Grapes	46
Kiwi fruit	52
Mango	55
Banana	55
Sultanas	56
Paw paw	58
Raisins	64
Pineapple	66
Cantaloupe melon	65
Watermelon	72

Vegetables

Carrots	49
Yam	51
Sweet potato	54
Sweetcorn	55
New potato	62
Beetroot	64
Swede	72
Pumpkin	75
Baked potato	85
Parsnips	97

BREAKFAST CEREALS

Kellogg's All-Bran ™	42
Porridge	42
Muesli (toasted)	43
Kellogg's Sultana Bran ™	52
Kellogg's Special K™	54
Oat bran	55
Muesli (untoasted)	56
Mini Wheats ™	58
Shredded Wheat™	67
Kellogg's Sustain™	68
Weetabix™	69
Grapenuts ™	71
Cheerios™	74
Kellogg's Coco Pops™	77
Kellogg's Rice Krispies™	82
Kellogg's Cornflakes™	84

BREADS/CRACKERS

Tortilla (wheat)	30
Pumpernickel	41
Heavy grain bread	47
Tortilla (corn)	52
Linseed rye	55
Pita bread	57
Cream crackers	65
Rye bread	65
Croissant	67
Ryvita	69
Crumpet	69
Fruit loaf (white)	69
Wholemeal bread	69
White bread	70
Melba toast	70
Bagel	72
Water biscuits	78
Puffed crispbread	81
Rice cakes	85
Baguette	95

GRAINS/PASTAS

Barley	25
Fettuccine	32
Vermicelli	35
Ravioli (meat)	39
Noodles (rice)	40
Spaghetti	41
Spirale (durum)	43
Macaroni	45
Linguine (thick)	46
Noodles (instant)	46
Bulgur wheat	48
Buckwheat	54
Linguine (thin)	55
Rice (basmati)	58
Couscous	65
Taco shells	68
Gnocchi	68
Rice (brown)	76
Rice (brown quick-cook)	80
Rice (white)	87
Rice (white, glutinous)	98

PULSES

Soya beans	18
Lentils (red)	26
Kidney beans	27
Lentils (green and brown)	30
Butter beans	31
Chickpeas	33
Haricot beans	38
Pinto beans	39
Baked beans	48
Broad beans	79

DAIRY FOODS

Yoghurt (with artificial sweetener)	14
Milk (full fat)	27
Milk (skimmed)	32
Yoghurt (low fat, fruit)	33
Custard	43
Ice cream (low fat)	50
Ice cream (full fat)	61

SNACK FOODS AND SWEETS

Peanuts	14
Corn chips	42
Fruit loaf (heavy)	47
Sponge cake	46
Chocolate	49
Crisps	54
Rich tea biscuits	55
Popcorn	55
Honey	58
Digestive biscuits	59
Muesli bar (commercial)	61
Shortbread	64
Table sugar	65
Mars ® bar	68
Waffles	76
Doughnut	76
Pretzels	83
Jelly beans	84

CONVENIENCE FOODS

Sausages	28
Fish fingers	38
Chicken nuggets	46
Pizza (cheese)	60
Chips	75

DRINKS

Apple juice (unsweetened)	40
Orange Juice	46
Pineapple Juice (unsweetened)	46
Grapefruit Juice (unsweetened)	48
Coca Cola ™	63
Orange squash (diluted)	66
Fanta™	68
Isostar	70
Gatorade	78
Lucozade ™	95

the recipes

The nutritional analysis given for each recipe refers to one serving, unless otherwise stated. The recipes in this book are specially designed to be:

Low GI

Low in fat

High in vitamins and minerals

Quick and easy to prepare

Easy to fit into your lifestyle

Practical – using everyday ingredients

Delicious!

morning muffins

170 g dried apricots, coarsely chopped

170 g unsweetened muesli

250 g self-raising flour

1 teaspoon baking powder

250 ml unsweetened apple juice

3 tablespoons vegetable oil

100 ml honey

1 large egg

a 12-hole muffin tin, lined with 12 paper cases

Makes 12

If when it comes to choosing between breakfast or an extra five minutes in bed, you choose the extra five minutes, this is the breakfast for you. Simply grab a muffin from an airtight container as you head out of the door and you have a healthy, filling breakfast that can be eaten on the move. On the odd occasion you have some time to spare, pop one in a warm oven for a couple of minutes, then serve it with a cup of freshly brewed coffee. It will take your breakfast times to an all new dimension.

Preparation time: 12 minutes

Put the apricots, muesli, flour and baking powder in a large mixing bowl and stir. In a separate bowl, mix the apple juice, oil, honey and egg. Fold into the dry ingredients, but do not overmix.

Spoon the mixture into the paper muffin cases. Bake in a preheated oven at 190°C (375°F) Gas 5 for 20 minutes, until golden and risen. Remove from the oven and serve immediately, or transfer to a wire rack to cool. Store in an airtight container for up to 3 days.

Variation: Add the finely grated zest of 1 unwaxed orange and replace the apple juice with freshly squeezed orange juice. Include the little shreds of orange flesh obtained from squeezing the fruit.

NUTRITIONAL INFORMATION
Kcal: **212**
Fat: **5 g (0.6 g saturated)**
Protein: **5 g**
Carbohydrate: **39 g**

extra oaty porridge

Porridge is one of the lowest-GI breakfasts you can eat. Research shows that oats can help lower your cholesterol, too. Although this recipe has a fairly high calorie content, it's a hearty breakfast that will keep you feeling full well up to lunchtime. Breakfast is the best time to eat a large amount of your daily calorie intake because it ensures you have plenty of energy to get you through the day.

50 g jumbo porridge oats

1 tablespoon oatmeal

300 ml skimmed milk, plus extra to serve (optional)

25 g sultanas, chopped dates or chopped dried figs

1 banana, sliced

2 teaspoons honey or maple syrup

1 teaspoon flaked almonds

Makes 1 large serving

Preparation time: 2–3 minutes

Put the oats, oatmeal and milk in a large microwaveable bowl and mix well. Cover and microwave on high for 4 minutes, stirring halfway through. Alternatively, put the oats, oatmeal and milk in a saucepan and cook over medium heat for 5 minutes, stirring continuously. Transfer to a serving bowl, add the sultanas, dates or figs, banana and extra milk, if using. Spoon over the honey or maple syrup, sprinkle with the almonds and serve.

Variation: Replace the almonds with finely chopped walnuts, hazelnuts or brazil nuts. Add slices of kiwi fruit or peach instead of the banana, if you prefer.

NUTRITIONAL INFORMATION
Kcal: **650**
Fat: **10 g (1.5 g saturated)**
Protein: **26 g**
Carbohydrate: **114 g**

all-in-one oats

This has got to be the king of all oat-based breakfasts. It's really quick to make, tastes superb, is packed full of essential vitamins, minerals and fibre and is guaranteed to keep you going right up until lunchtime and beyond. Leaving the mixture in the refrigerator overnight gives the oats time to absorb the flavours of the dried fruit, apple and nuts and develop a smooth, creamy texture from the milk.

Base mixture

8 tablespoons oats

1 tablespoon chopped dried apricots

1 tablespoon sultanas

1 tablespoon finely chopped walnuts

1 tablespoon finely chopped almonds, brazil nuts or hazelnuts

To serve *(per person)*

½ apple, grated

150–300 ml skimmed milk

4 raspberries

4 blueberries

4 grapes

½ kiwi fruit, sliced

1 tablespoon low-fat yoghurt (optional)

Serves 4

Preparation time: 10 minutes

Put the oats, dried apricots, sultanas and nuts in an airtight container, shake well and reserve. The night before you want to serve this for breakfast, pour about 3 tablespoons of the mixture into a large bowl. Add the grated apple and 150 ml milk. Stir well.

Cover and leave in the refrigerator overnight. Just before serving, add a little more skimmed milk to loosen the mixture, if you like. Add the raspberries, blueberries, grapes and kiwi fruit. Serve topped with 1 tablespoon of low-fat yoghurt, if using.

Variation: You can serve this breakfast topped with almost any fruit. So experiment with bananas, mangoes, oranges, papayas, peaches, pears or plums, depending on what's in season and to get just the flavour you like.

NUTRITIONAL INFORMATION
Kcal: **465**
Fat: **10 g (1.5 g saturated)**
Protein: **20 g**
Carbohydrate: **75 g**

breakfast bars

Forget shop-bought cereal bars. These are the real thing and once you've tasted the difference there's no going back. They are really easy to throw together and make a great snack at any time of the day.

200 g stoneground wholemeal flour

75 g light muscovado sugar

2 teaspoons baking powder

1 teaspoon ground cinnamon

1 teaspoon mixed spice

1/2 teaspoon ground ginger

1/2 teaspoon sea salt

150 g rolled oats

160 g dried apricots, finely chopped

70 g sunflower seeds

175 ml unsweetened apple sauce

100 ml unsweetened apple juice

3 eggs

2 teaspoons vegetable oil

a shallow cake tin, 20 x 30 cm, greased and base lined

Makes 16

Preparation time: 15 minutes

Put the flour, sugar, baking powder, spices and salt in a large bowl. Mix well. Stir in the oats, apricots and sunflower seeds. In a separate bowl, mix the apple sauce, apple juice, eggs and oil. Add to the flour mixture and stir until well mixed.

Pour into the lined cake tin and press down with the back of a spoon. Bake in a preheated oven at 200°C (400°F) Gas 6 for 15–20 minutes, until lightly browned. Remove from the oven and let cool in the tin before cutting into 16 bars. Store in an airtight container for up to 3 days.

Variation: Mix 2 tablespoons of jumbo oats with 1 tablespoon of flaked almonds and sprinkle on top just before baking, if you like.

NUTRITIONAL INFORMATION
Kcal: **143**
Fat: **3.7 g (0.5 g saturated)**
Protein: **5 g**
Carbohydrate: **23 g**

kickstart kebabs

These kebabs are a great alternative to fruit salad. They work just as well cooked on a barbecue and served as a dessert in the summer. Feel free to experiment using your favourite fruits to get just the taste you like.

2 small bananas, sliced

freshly squeezed juice of 1 lemon

8 cubes of canned pineapple in fruit juice, drained

1 large orange, peeled and divided into segments

8 pitted prunes

8 dried apricots

2 tablespoons freshly squeezed orange juice

1 tablespoon clear honey

½ teaspoon ground mixed spice

low-fat natural yoghurt, to serve

4 long wooden skewers, soaked in water for 10 minutes

Makes 4

Preparation time: 10 minutes

Put the banana slices in a shallow bowl, sprinkle with the lemon juice and toss gently to prevent them from browning. Thread the bananas, pineapple, orange segments, prunes and apricots onto the 4 skewers, dividing the ingredients equally between them.

Put the orange juice, honey and mixed spice in a small bowl and mix. Brush this mixture over the fruit skewers. Cook the kebabs under a preheated medium-hot grill for 5 minutes, turning frequently. Brush with any remaining orange juice mixture while they are cooking to prevent them from drying out. Serve warm, with some low-fat natural yoghurt.

Variation: Use other fresh, canned and dried fruits of your choice, such as pink grapefruit, peaches, kiwi fruit, pears and large raisins. Use pineapple or apple juice in place of the orange juice. Use ground cinnamon or nutmeg instead of the mixed spice.

NUTRITIONAL INFORMATION
Kcal: **241**
Fat: **1 g (0 g saturated)**
Protein: **5 g**
Carbohydrate: **57 g**

hot pear pancakes

This is a favourite breakfast choice among children and adults alike. There's something quite indulgent about the combination of the hot pancakes, pears and crème fraîche. If this breakfast doesn't cheer you up on a cold, grey morning, nothing will.

NUTRITIONAL INFORMATION

Kcal: **333**
Fat: **7 g (0.7 g saturated)**
Protein: **12 g**
Carbohydrate: **61 g**

Preparation time: 18 minutes

6 ripe pears, cored and sliced

150 ml water

100 g stoneground wholemeal flour

2 teaspoons baking powder

175 g fine oatmeal

475 ml skimmed milk

2 eggs

1 tablespoon sunflower oil

To serve

1 teaspoon ground cinnamon

a handful of blueberries, raspberries or chopped strawberries

freshly squeezed juice of 1 lemon

half-fat crème fraîche

fresh mint leaves (optional)

Serves 6

Put the pears and water in a saucepan and heat until simmering. Reduce the heat and let simmer gently until the pears are softened, 3–5 minutes. Drain the pears and keep them warm in a low oven. Reserve the cooking water.

To make the pancakes, sift the flour and baking powder into a bowl and stir in the oatmeal. Make a well in the centre of the mixture. Put the milk and eggs in a separate bowl and beat well. Pour into the dry ingredients and whisk with a hand-held whisk to form a smooth, thick batter.

Heat a large, non-stick frying pan until hot. Add 1 teaspoon of oil, carefully swirl the pan until lightly coated then drain, reserving the oil. Pour in a little batter to form a small pancake. Cook for 2 minutes, until the bubbles on the surface start to burst. Turn over using a spatula and cook for a further 2 minutes, until cooked through. Transfer the pancakes to a plate, stacking them between layers of baking parchment. Keep them warm in a low oven, while making the rest.

To serve, put 1 pancake on a serving plate, top with 2–3 pear slices, sprinkle with a little cinnamon, a few fresh berries, a squeeze of lemon juice and some of the cooking water from the pears. Put another pancake on top. Repeat the layers once more, then top with a spoonful of crème fraîche and a few mint leaves, if using. Serve immediately.

Variation: Use stoned, chopped fresh plums or sliced bananas instead of the pears. You could make a savoury version with scrambled eggs and chopped tomatoes instead of the fruit, or sautéed mushrooms with fresh herbs and a little half-fat crème fraîche.

french toast

When I was a child, my mother made me French toast as a special breakfast treat. To keep the GI of the meal low, use really grainy, nutty bread. Plain wholemeal bread doesn't count; with a GI value of 69 it is only one point lower than white bread (GI 70).

2 eggs, lightly beaten

4 thick slices stoneground wholemeal or wholegrain bread, cut in half diagonally

sunflower oil, for frying

a handful of fresh chives, snipped

sea salt and freshly ground black pepper

Serves 2

Preparation time: 2 minutes

Put the eggs in a shallow dish, season with salt and pepper and beat well.

Soak 2 triangles of bread in the egg mixture, turning once to coat well. Heat a large, non-stick frying pan until hot and brush with a little oil. Put the soaked bread in the pan and cook for 2 minutes, until golden brown and crisp. Flip the bread over and cook for a further 2 minutes.

Transfer the toast to a plate and keep it warm in a low oven while you cook the remaining slices. Serve warm, sprinkled with the chives.

Variation: For a sweet teatime treat, add 1 teaspoon of ground cinnamon to the egg mixture and replace the chives with a few fresh berries.

NUTRITIONAL INFORMATION
Kcal: **314**
Fat: **9 g (2 g saturated)**
Protein: **17 g**
Carbohydrate: **37 g**

bacon, tomato and basil toasty

Everyone loves a bacon sandwich and this is a really healthy, quick and easy version. The combination of hot tomato, fresh basil and sizzling bacon makes a fabulous breakfast or lunch.

2 slices extra-lean bacon

1 tomato, sliced

1 thick slice stoneground wholemeal or wholegrain bread

2 teaspoons chopped fresh basil leaves

sea salt and freshly ground black pepper

Serves 1

Preparation time: 3 minutes

Put the bacon slices on a grill tray and cook under a preheated hot grill for 2 minutes. Add the tomato slices to the tray and cook for a further 2 minutes. Turn the bacon over and add the slice of bread to the tray. Let the bread turn golden brown on one side before turning over and lightly toasting the other side.

Remove the grill tray from the heat. Put the bacon on the lightly toasted side of the bread, top with the tomato slices and basil, then season to taste with salt and pepper. Return the grill tray to the heat and cook for a further 2 minutes. Serve immediately.

Variation: For a quick lunchtime snack, rub the bread with a halved garlic clove before toasting, then cut the garlic clove into thin slivers and insert into the tomato slices, then grill. Put the tomatoes on top of the bread, sprinkle with some Parmesan cheese shavings and serve with a green salad.

NUTRITIONAL INFORMATION
Kcal: **243**
Fat: **9 g (3 g saturated)**
Protein: **19 g**
Carbohydrate: **21 g**

scrambled egg with smoked salmon

This dish contains just slightly more than 30 per cent fat, but don't worry because much of the fat comes from the salmon, which is a great source of omega-3 fatty acids. Research shows that if you eat oily fish, such as salmon, trout, mackerel and sardines, three times a week, you can lower the risk of suffering from a fatal heart attack by as much as 40 per cent! So tuck in and feel free to replace the salmon with a hot smoked kipper or grilled peppered mackerel, if you fancy a change.

Preparation time: 3–4 minutes

Put the egg, milk, half the parsley or chives and a little salt and pepper in a microwaveable bowl and beat well. Microwave on high for 2 minutes, stirring halfway through. Alternatively, put the beaten egg mixture in a non-stick saucepan and cook over low heat, stirring continuously, until the egg begins to set.

Spoon the scrambled egg onto the toast. Top with the smoked salmon and sprinkle with the remaining parsley or chives. Serve immediately with a wedge of lemon, if using.

Variation: Add 1 ripe medium chopped tomato to the egg at the end of cooking.

1 large free-range egg

50 ml skimmed milk

1 tablespoon chopped fresh flat leaf parsley or snipped chives

1 slice stoneground wholemeal or wholegrain bread, toasted

2 slices smoked salmon

sea salt and freshly ground black pepper

lemon wedge, to serve (optional)

Serves 1

NUTRITIONAL INFORMATION
Kcal: **260**
Fat: **10 g (2.6 g saturated)**
Protein: **26 g**
Carbohydrate: **16 g**

kedgeree

This classic English breakfast dish is great whatever time of day you choose to make it. This recipe uses basmati rice; with a GI of 58, it keeps you feeling energized and sustained for much longer than if quick-cook white rice was used, which can have a GI as high as 98.

Preparation time: 12–15 minutes

Put the haddock, bay leaves and water in a frying pan and bring to the boil. Cover, reduce the heat and simmer for 5 minutes. Remove the pan from the heat, drain and, when cool enough to handle, remove the skin from the fish and flake the flesh with a fork. Set aside.

Meanwhile, bring a large saucepan of water to the boil. Add the rice and return to the boil. Stir, then reduce the heat and simmer for 10 minutes, until the rice is cooked but still has a slight bite to it. Drain and reserve.

Heat a large, non-stick frying pan. Add the oil, spring onions and garlic and fry gently until softened and slightly coloured, about 6 minutes. Add the curry powder and cook for 2 minutes. Add the lemon juice, the reserved haddock and rice. Cut one egg into wedges and reserve. Chop the other one into small pieces and add to the pan. Sprinkle with the coriander and season to taste with pepper. Continue to heat, stirring gently, until piping hot.

Transfer the kedgeree to a warm serving dish. Top with the egg and lemon wedges and serve immediately.

Variation: Use 400 g fresh salmon fillets instead of the haddock and cook as above. Alternatively, add 75 g smoked salmon, cut into thin strips, at the same time as the chopped egg.

NUTRITIONAL INFORMATION
Kcal: **372**
Fat: **12 g (2 g saturated)**
Protein: **34 g**
Carbohydrate: **26 g**

450 g undyed smoked haddock fillets

2 bay leaves

100 ml water

120 g basmati rice

3 tablespoons olive oil

5 spring onions, finely chopped

1–2 garlic cloves, finely chopped

1–1½ tablespoons curry powder

freshly squeezed juice of 1 lemon

2 hard-boiled eggs

2 tablespoons chopped fresh coriander

freshly ground black pepper

lemon wedges, to serve

Serves 4

smoothies

Smoothies are a winner for breakfast. They are so quick to prepare and are a delicious way of increasing your intake of fruit – and all the vitamins, minerals and immune-boosting antioxidants that fruit contains.

tropical treat

½ ripe mango, peeled and chopped

1 banana, chopped

100 ml freshly squeezed orange juice

1 passion fruit, halved

Serves 1

Preparation time: 3 minutes

Put the mango, banana and orange juice in a blender and blend until smooth. Add the passion fruit pulp and seeds and stir. If the smoothie is too thick, add some extra orange juice to thin. Pour into a glass and serve.

> **NUTRITIONAL INFORMATION**
> Kcal: **175**
> Fat: **0 g**
> Protein: **3 g**
> Carbohydrate: **43 g**

banana magic

150 g fresh or frozen mixed berries, for example strawberries, raspberries, blueberries

1 banana, chopped

150 ml low-fat strawberry or raspberry yoghurt

120 ml unsweetened apple or orange juice (optional)

1 teaspoon honey (optional)

Serves 1

blueberry blast

75 g blueberries

1 small banana, chopped

150 ml unsweetened apple juice

Serves 1

Preparation time: 3 minutes

Put the blueberries, banana and apple juice in a blender and blend until smooth. Pour into a glass and serve.

> **NUTRITIONAL INFORMATION**
> Kcal: **209**
> Fat: **0 g**
> Protein: **3 g**
> Carbohydrate: **51 g**

Preparation time: 3 minutes

Put the berries, banana and yoghurt in a blender. If using frozen fruits, add the unsweetened apple or orange juice. Blend until smooth. Add 1 teaspoon honey, according to taste. Pour into a glass and serve.

> **NUTRITIONAL INFORMATION**
> Kcal: **268**
> Fat: **1 g (0.6 g saturated)**
> Protein: **8 g**
> Carbohydrate: **56 g**

lunchboxes and snacks

chicken and hommus wraps

The hommus in these wraps is a great source of monounsaturated fat – the sort that not only lowers your bad cholesterol (or low-density lipoproteins), but maintains and may even increase your good cholesterol (or high-density lipoproteins). The tortillas, with a GI rating of approximately 30, make a great alternative to rye or wholegrain breads.

2 tablespoons hommus (see page 99)

4 small tortillas

1 large grilled chicken breast, cut into thin strips

½ small cucumber, cut lengthways into thin strips

4 medium cos or romaine lettuce leaves, shredded

4 teaspoons chilli oil or sweet chilli sauce

sea salt and freshly ground black pepper

4 cocktail sticks

Serves 2

Preparation time: 10 minutes

Spread ½ tablespoon of hommus over each tortilla. Put the strips of chicken and cucumber on top of the hommus, then top with the shredded lettuce.

Drizzle each wrap with 1 teaspoon of chilli oil or sweet chilli sauce and season generously with salt and pepper. Carefully roll up the tortillas and secure each one in place with a cocktail stick. Chill the wraps in the refrigerator until you are ready to eat.

Variation: If you prefer a vegetarian alternative, use tomato slices and rocket leaves instead of the chicken.

NUTRITIONAL INFORMATION

Kcal: **592**
Fat: **12 g (2 g saturated)**
Protein: **52 g**
Carbohydrate: **70 g**

sandwiches

Whether they are made from white or wholemeal bread, baguettes or bagels, sandwiches are the number one choice for lunch. However, the high-GI rating of all these types of bread (baguettes have a GI as high as 95) results in many of us experiencing that dreaded mid-afternoon energy slump, where we feel tired, lack concentration and crave something sweet. These three sandwiches all use linseed rye bread, a much slower energy-releasing alternative to many other breads. They are also low in fat. So try one of these instead of your usual egg mayonnaise sandwich or cream cheese bagel and look forward to feeling energized all afternoon.

cottage cheese, ham and apple

2 tablespoons cottage cheese

2 teaspoons freshly snipped chives

1 slice lean ham, cut in half

2 slices linseed rye bread

½ apple, rinsed, cored and thinly sliced

sea salt and freshly ground black pepper

Serves 1

Preparation time: 3–4 minutes

Put the cottage cheese and chives in a bowl. Season with salt and pepper to taste and mix well. Put 1 half slice of ham on each slice of bread, spread with the cottage cheese and top with the apple slices. Cut in half, to serve.

Variation: You can use a nutty, wholegrain bread as an alternative to the linseed rye bread in any of these sandwiches.

NUTRITIONAL INFORMATION
Kcal: 342
Fat: 8 g (3 g saturated)
Protein: 29 g
Carbohydrate: 40 g

cambozola and grapes

25 g Cambozola cheese

2 slices linseed rye bread

12 seedless grapes, halved

Serves 1

Preparation time: 2 minutes

Spread the Cambozola thinly on each piece of rye bread and put the halved grapes on top. Cut in half, to serve.

NUTRITIONAL INFORMATION
Kcal: 283
Fat: 8 g (5 g saturated)
Protein: 10 g
Carbohydrate: 39 g

turkey and cranberry

a small handful of baby spinach leaves, lightly rinsed

2 slices linseed rye bread

1–2 thin slices turkey breast

1–2 teaspoons cranberry sauce

Serves 1

Preparation time: 3–4 minutes

Divide the spinach leaves between the 2 slices of rye bread and put the turkey slices on top. Put 1 teaspoon of cranberry sauce on the turkey. Cut in half, to serve.

NUTRITIONAL INFORMATION
Kcal: 256
Fat: 1.5 g (0 g saturated)
Protein: 17 g
Carbohydrate: 45 g

tangy pita pockets

Pita bread has a lower GI than most breads and it is really quick and easy to use. It can be toasted from frozen in minutes, so if you keep some wholemeal pita breads in your freezer, you are only ever minutes away from a healthy, low-GI lunch or snack.

1 wholemeal pita bread

a handful of baby spinach leaves, lightly rinsed

2 slices beef tomato

1 slice extra-lean ham

Salsa

5 cm piece cucumber, finely chopped

½ red chilli, deseeded and finely chopped

1 medium tomato, finely chopped

a handful of fresh coriander, chopped

freshly squeezed juice of ½ lemon

1 teaspoon olive oil

sea salt and freshly ground black pepper

Serves 1

Preparation time: 5 minutes

To make the salsa, put the cucumber, chilli, tomato, coriander, lemon juice, oil and salt and pepper, to taste, in a bowl and mix.

Warm the pita bread under a preheated hot grill until it rises in the middle, about 2 minutes. Split in half and fill with the spinach leaves, tomato slices, ham and 1 tablespoon of salsa. Refrigerate until ready to eat.

Variation: Fill the pita with 1 tablespoon of hommus (see page 99), a few salad leaves, some sliced cucumber and thinly shredded spring onions.

NUTRITIONAL INFORMATION
Kcal: **257**
Fat: **3 g (0 g saturated)**
Protein: **14 g**
Carbohydrate: **50 g**

spicy lentil dip

Lentils have a very low-GI rating (26) and are a good source of protein and fibre, and contain lots of potassium, zinc and folic acid. They are very filling, too, so they make an ideal base for a snack or meal.

125 g red lentils

400 ml water

25 g polyunsaturated margarine

1 small onion, finely chopped

1–2 tablespoons curry powder

sea salt and freshly ground black pepper

To serve

chopped fresh coriander

vegetable crudités, such as baby carrots, baby peppers or radishes

wholemeal pita bread, griddled (optional)

Serves 6

Preparation time: 15 minutes

Put the lentils and water in a saucepan. Bring to the boil, reduce the heat and simmer for 20–30 minutes, until the water is absorbed. Remove from the heat and mash with a fork.

Melt the margarine in a small saucepan, add the onion and cook gently for about 5 minutes, until soft but not coloured. Add the curry powder and cook for a further 1–2 minutes. Add the mashed lentils to the pan, stir and cook for 5 minutes more. Season with salt and pepper, to taste.

Remove the pan from the heat. If you prefer a smooth texture, put the lentil mixture in a blender or food processor and blend until smooth. If the dip is a bit dry, add a couple of teaspoons of water to moisten. Alternatively, for a chunkier texture, leave the mixture as it is.

Let cool. Sprinkle with coriander and serve with your choice of vegetable crudités and strips of griddled pita bread, if using.

Variation: Use Puy lentils instead of the red lentils. They will need to be cooked for slightly longer, a further 15–20 minutes. Replace the curry powder with 1 teaspoon of *herbes de Provence* and add 2 tablespoons of shredded fresh basil leaves at the end of cooking. Puy lentils retain their shape so this will make a chunkier dip.

NUTRITIONAL INFORMATION
Kcal: **106**
Fat: **3.5 g (0.7 g saturated)**
Protein: **6 g**
Carbohydrate: **14 g**

tuscan salad

By adding high-protein foods, such as chicken, fish and meat, to a meal, you naturally lower its overall GI rating. That's why this combination of tuna and haricot beans (GI 38) is a great way to avoid that mid-afternoon energy slump that often sees you reaching for a fatty, sugary snack to keep you going. Net result? You'll naturally take in fewer calories and less fat, which can only be a good thing for your health – and your waistline.

400 g canned haricot beans, drained and rinsed

400 g canned kidney beans, drained and rinsed

1 red onion, finely chopped

2 tablespoons pitted green olives

4 tomatoes, chopped

1 avocado, peeled, stoned and cut into cubes

370 g canned tuna in spring water, drained and lightly flaked

a few chives or chive flowers, to serve

Dressing

1 teaspoon wholegrain mustard

2 tablespoons extra virgin olive oil

4 tablespoons balsamic vinegar

2–3 garlic cloves, crushed

2 tablespoons finely snipped chives

2 tablespoons chopped fresh tarragon

2 tablespoons chopped fresh flat leaf parsley

sea salt and freshly ground black pepper

Serves 4

Preparation time: 15 minutes

To make the dressing, put the mustard, oil, vinegar, garlic, chives, tarragon and parsley in a large bowl and mix well. Season with salt and pepper, to taste.

Add the haricot and kidney beans, onion, olives, tomatoes, avocado and tuna to the dressing. Mix well. Serve in individual bowls, sprinkled with some chives or chive flowers.

Variation: Give this salad a fruity twist by replacing the balsamic vinegar in the dressing with raspberry vinegar. Scatter a few fresh raspberries over the salad just before serving.

NUTRITIONAL INFORMATION
Kcal: **584**
Fat: **16 g (2.8 g saturated)**
Protein: **52 g**
Carbohydrate: **64 g**

chicken, apple and peanut salad

Peanuts are nutritional powerhouses. Not only do they provide you with eight vitamins and 13 minerals – including some that are hard to find naturally, such as magnesium and zinc – they contain plant chemicals, such as beta-sitosterol, which can help to protect against cancer. Research also shows that eating nuts more than five times per week reduces the risk of coronary heart disease by 18–51 per cent.

2 apples, cored and chopped

1 tablespoon freshly squeezed lemon juice

100 g baby spinach leaves, lightly rinsed

300 g grilled chicken breast, chopped

1 tablespoon unsalted roasted peanuts

4 tomatoes, chopped

½ small cucumber, chopped

2 tablespoons balsamic vinegar

sea salt and freshly ground black pepper

1 lemon, cut into wedges, to serve (optional)

Serves 4

Preparation time: 12–15 minutes

Put the apple pieces in a large bowl, sprinkle with the lemon juice and toss to coat. Add the spinach leaves, chicken, peanuts, tomatoes and cucumber.

Pour the balsamic vinegar over the salad, season with salt and pepper and toss well. Serve with lemon wedges, if using.

Variation: This salad tastes great with flaked smoked mackerel fillets instead of the chicken.

NUTRITIONAL INFORMATION
Kcal: **216**
Fat: **6 g (1.3 g saturated)**
Protein: **30 g**
Carbohydrate: **10 g**

chicken and chilli chickpea salad

The great thing about this salad is you can eat it any time of the day, hot or cold. Because the beans hold their shape, it travels well, too. So if you make a bit too much for supper, just throw it in an airtight container and take it with you the next day for lunch.

NUTRITIONAL INFORMATION
Kcal: **233**
Fat: **6 g (2 g saturated)**
Protein: **29 g**
Carbohydrate: **20 g**

400 g canned chickpeas, drained and rinsed

100 g canned red kidney beans, drained and rinsed

1 red onion, finely chopped

2 fresh red chillies, deseeded and finely chopped

2 tablespoons fresh basil leaves, torn

1½ tablespoons chopped fresh flat leaf parsley

a small bunch of chives, finely chopped

250 g grilled chicken breast, chopped

250 g very ripe cherry tomatoes, halved

5 cm piece cucumber, chopped

fresh Parmesan cheese shavings

warm pita bread, to serve (optional)

Dressing

2 tablespoons extra virgin olive oil

4 tablespoons balsamic vinegar

2–3 garlic cloves, crushed

1 teaspoon wholegrain mustard

sea salt and freshly ground black pepper

Serves 4

Preparation time: 20 minutes

To make the dressing, put the oil, vinegar, garlic and mustard in a salad bowl. Season with salt and pepper, to taste, and stir to mix. Add the chickpeas, kidney beans, onion, chillies and herbs and mix well. Cover and chill in the refrigerator for 2–4 hours to let the flavours infuse.

When ready to eat, add the chicken, tomatoes and cucumber to the salad. Season with salt and pepper, to taste, and toss well. Sprinkle with a few shavings of Parmesan and serve with warm pita bread, if using.

Variation: Replace the chicken with turkey breast steaks. Chop them into cubes, then marinate for 30 minutes in 2 tablespoons of freshly squeezed lime juice mixed with 1 beaten egg white, 1 tablespoon of finely grated lime zest and ½–1 teaspoon of crushed dried chillies. Grill the turkey steaks or cook on a preheated stove-top grill pan for 5 minutes on each side. Add the cooked turkey to the chickpea salad when ready to serve. Replace the basil with freshly chopped coriander.

roasted vegetables

It takes just minutes to throw these vegetables and herbs in a roasting tin, then you can forget about them for 30 or 40 minutes while the heat of the oven brings out all their lovely flavours. This is a great way of increasing your intake of fresh vegetables and it goes with anything – fish, meat, rice or pasta. It tastes great hot or cold, so it's perfect for your lunchbox.

1 red onion, cut into wedges

250 g courgettes, thickly sliced

225 g baby corn

225 g aubergine, cut into large chunks

1 red pepper, deseeded and cut into large chunks

1 yellow pepper, deseeded and cut into large chunks

16 cherry tomatoes

2–4 garlic cloves, thinly sliced

1 red chilli, deseeded and chopped (optional)

1½ tablespoons olive oil

2 tablespoons chopped fresh basil leaves

1 tablespoon chopped fresh rosemary

balsamic vinegar, for drizzling

sea salt and freshly ground black pepper

Serves 4

Preparation time: 12–15 minutes

Put the onion, courgettes, corn, aubergine, peppers, tomatoes, garlic and chilli, if using, in a large non-stick roasting tin. Sprinkle with the oil, season with salt and pepper and toss until all the vegetables are lightly coated with the oil. Don't be tempted to add any more oil as the vegetables will release plenty of juices when cooking. Shake the tin gently to make the vegetables lie in a single layer.

Roast in a preheated oven at 220°C (425°F) Gas 7 for 30–40 minutes, turning once or twice during cooking, until the vegetables are beginning to brown at the edges.

Remove from the oven, sprinkle with the basil and rosemary and toss well. Drizzle over a little balsamic vinegar and serve.

Variation: Add 200 g chopped, grilled lean bacon or ham to the vegetables once cooked. (This will add an extra 80 Kcals and 2 g fat per serving). Use a flavoured oil, such as chilli oil or herb oil, instead of the olive oil to add a stronger flavour. Experiment with different herbs, such as parsley or chives, to vary the flavour.

> **NUTRITIONAL INFORMATION**
> Kcal: **84**
> Fat: **3 g (0 g saturated)**
> Protein: **3 g**
> Carbohydrate: **11 g**

herby cheese swirls

Hot or cold, these make a great snack either mid-morning or mid-afternoon. Don't be tempted to load them up with butter or high-fat cheeses. Use low-fat cottage cheese, low-fat cream cheese, hoummus or sliced tomatoes and basil, instead.

NUTRITIONAL INFORMATION

Kcal: **119**
Fat: **3.5 g (1 g saturated)**
Protein: **5.25 g**
Carbohydrate: **17 g**

150 g wholemeal self-raising flour

2 teaspoons baking powder

100 g unprocessed oat bran

30 g polyunsaturated margarine

125 ml skimmed milk

50–60 ml water

60 g low-fat Cheddar cheese, grated

1 tablespoon chopped fresh flat leaf parsley

2 tablespoons chopped fresh basil leaves

2 teaspoons chopped fresh rosemary

To serve (optional)

low-fat cottage cheese

low-fat cream cheese

hoummus (see page 99)

tomato slices and fresh basil leaves

a baking sheet

Makes 10

Preparation time: 15 minutes

Sift the flour and the baking powder into a large bowl, then stir in the oat bran. Chop the margarine into small pieces, then add it to the dry ingredients. Rub it into the dry mixture using the tips of your fingers, until the mixture resembles breadcrumbs. Make a well in the centre and add the milk and half the water. Mix lightly with a round-bladed knife, adding extra water if necessary, to make a soft, pliable dough. Do not overmix.

Turn the dough out onto a lightly floured surface and knead gently. Roll out the dough to a rectangle about 1 cm thick. Scatter half the cheese and all the herbs evenly over the surface, then dampen the edges of the dough with water. Beginning from one long side, roll up the dough like a Swiss roll, to make a thick sausage shape. Carefully cut into 3 cm slices using a sharp knife, to make about 10 rounds.

Transfer the rounds to a baking sheet, spacing them well apart. Sprinkle with the remaining cheese and bake in a preheated oven at 200°C (400°F) Gas 6 for 15–20 minutes, until golden. Serve hot or cold, either plain or with your choice of topping.

Variation: Roll the dough out on a lightly floured surface to a thickness of 5 cm. Cut into 7.5 cm rounds. Sprinkle with the grated cheese and bake as above. Cut in half and top with some low-fat spread, 1 teaspoon of low-fat fromage frais and a slice of tomato.

peanut butter bars

Yes, peanuts are high in fat, but it's the healthy, unsaturated sort. Also, we're using such a small quantity of peanut butter here in relation to the other ingredients that the overall percentage of fat in the bars remains low. Peanuts are a good source of plant sterols, which can block absorption of cholesterol in the body and hence lower your blood cholesterol levels. And while we're on the subject of peanuts, did you know that they are in fact not nuts at all? They are part of the legume family and therefore have many of the beneficial properties of beans, including being high in fibre and having one of the lowest-GI ratings you can find. So it's no wonder these bars are so filling – they are almost a meal in themselves!

4 tablespoons crunchy peanut butter

4 tablespoons clear honey

100 g jumbo oats

75 g porridge oats

50 g sultanas

1 tablespoon stoneground wholemeal flour

a non-stick cake tin, 23 x 15 cm

Makes 8 bars

NUTRITIONAL INFORMATION
Kcal: **205**
Fat: **6 g (1.4 g saturated)**
Protein: **6 g**
Carbohydrate: **31 g**

Preparation time: 10–12 minutes

Put the peanut butter and honey in a saucepan and heat very gently until melted, about 4 minutes. Add the oats, sultanas and flour and stir well until thoroughly mixed and the mixture has the consistency of crumbs.

Pour the mixture into the cake tin and press in with the back of a spoon. Bake in a preheated oven at 190°C (375°F) Gas 5 for 15 minutes. Leave in the tin until cool, then cut into bars. Leave until completely cold before removing from the tin. The bars can be stored in an airtight container for up to 2 weeks.

Variation: Substitute the sultanas for raisins or chopped dried apricots.

apricot flapjack

These are a favourite with children and adults alike. They keep and travel really well, so they are great to take with you when you are out and about.

100 g low-fat polyunsaturated margarine

150 g golden syrup

140 g jumbo oats

100 g porridge oats

75 g dried apricots, chopped

75 g sultanas

a non-stick cake tin, 18 x 28 cm

Makes 14

Preparation time: 10 minutes

Put the margarine and syrup in a saucepan and heat gently until the margarine is melted. Add the oats, apricots and sultanas and stir well to mix. Transfer the mixture to the cake tin and press down evenly with the back of a large spoon.

Bake in the middle of a preheated oven at 190°C (375°F) Gas 5 for 20 minutes, until golden brown. Remove from the oven and let the flapjacks cool in the tin. When cold, cut into squares. Store in an airtight container for up to 5 days.

Variation: Replace the dried apricots with finely chopped dried fruit salad, dried cranberries or dried blueberries.

NUTRITIONAL INFORMATION
Kcal: **133**
Fat: **3 g (1 g saturated)**
Protein: **2.5 g**
Carbohydrate: **23 g**

nutty oat biscuits

Most biscuits you can buy from the supermarket are made with highly refined, high-GI flour and lots of saturated fat. These, however, keep the fat content and the GI low by using a small amount of oil and a combination of wholemeal flour and oatmeal.

75 g stoneground wholemeal flour

150 g medium oatmeal

1 teaspoon vanilla extract

2 tablespoons sunflower oil

50 g light muscovado sugar

50 g raisins, chopped

1 large egg, lightly beaten

a baking sheet, lightly greased

Makes 12

Preparation time: 10 minutes

Put the flour, oatmeal, vanilla extract, oil, sugar, raisins and beaten egg in a large bowl and mix well.

Put 1 large tablespoon of the mixture onto the prepared baking sheet and flatten to a 7.5 cm round with a spatula or the back of a spoon. Repeat with the rest of the mixture, spacing the biscuits well apart on the baking sheet.

Bake in a preheated oven at 180°C (350°F) Gas 4 for 10 minutes, or until the biscuits are firm to the touch.

Remove from the oven and let cool on the baking sheet for about 2 minutes, or until firm enough to transfer to a wire rack to cool completely. Store in an airtight container for up to 1 week.

Variation: Replace the vanilla extract with the finely grated zest of 1 unwaxed orange and sprinkle the tops of the biscuits with a few toasted chopped hazelnuts before baking.

NUTRITIONAL INFORMATION
Kcal: **118**
Fat: **3 g** (0.4 g saturated)
Protein: **3 g**
Carbohydrate: **20 g**

wholewheat cinnamon fruit scones

Everyone loves a warm scone and the combination of cinnamon and dried fruit makes these extra special. Make sure you sieve the flour to keep them as light as possible and give the oven plenty of time to heat up before you bake them to ensure they rise properly.

150 g wholewheat flour, plus extra for dusting

150 g self-raising flour

2 teaspoons baking powder

3–4 teaspoons ground cinnamon

50 g demerara sugar

50 g polyunsaturated margarine

80 g mixed dried fruit

2 eggs

about 2 tablespoons skimmed milk, plus extra for brushing

To serve

low-fat spread

sliced strawberries (optional)

a baking sheet, lightly greased

Makes 6

Preparation time: 10 minutes

Sift the flours into a mixing bowl, adding any bran left in the sieve to the bowl. Add the baking powder, cinnamon and sugar and stir. Chop the margarine into small pieces, then add it to the dry ingredients. Rub it into the dry mixture using the tips of your fingers. The mixture should resemble breadcrumbs. Stir in the dried fruit.

In a separate bowl, beat the eggs with 2 tablespoons of milk. Add this to the flour mixture, mixing it to a smooth dough with a round-bladed knife. Bring the dough together with your hands. If the mixture is too dry, add a little more milk.

Transfer the dough to a lightly floured work surface. Roll out to a thickness of 2.5 cm and cut out rounds using a 6.5 cm diameter cutter. Transfer the rounds to the prepared baking sheet, brush the tops with milk and dust them lightly with wholewheat flour.

Bake on a high shelf in a preheated oven at 230°C (450°F) Gas 8 for about 15 minutes, until well risen and golden. Remove from the oven. Serve warm or cold, split in half and topped with low-fat spread and some sliced strawberries, if using.

Variation: Serve topped with a few halved grapes. For an extra special treat, spread sparingly with a little strawberry jam and top with 1 teaspoon half-fat crème fraîche and some sliced fresh strawberries.

> **NUTRITIONAL INFORMATION**
> Kcal: **122**
> Fat: **4 g** (0.8 g saturated)
> Protein: **4 g**
> Carbohydrate: **19 g**

date and walnut bars

These tasty bars couldn't be simpler to make. Just throw all the ingredients in a bowl, spoon it onto a baking sheet and 25 minutes later you can look forward to taking them out of the oven.

225 g wholemeal self-raising flour

1 teaspoon ground cinnamon

2 tablespoons sunflower oil

75 g light muscovado sugar

1 large egg, lightly beaten

200 ml skimmed milk

175 g dates, chopped

50 g walnuts, chopped

a shallow, non-stick baking tin, 18 x 28 cm

Makes 12

Preparation time: 10 minutes.

Put the flour, cinnamon, oil, sugar, beaten egg and milk in a large bowl and mix well to give a smooth consistency. Stir in the dates and walnuts.

Spoon the mixture into the baking tin and smooth the top with a spatula. Bake in a preheated oven at 180°C (350°F) Gas 4 for 20–25 minutes, until golden brown. Remove from the oven and let cool in the tin. When cool, cut into bars. Store in an airtight container for up to 5 days.

Variation: Use only 50 g light muscovado sugar in the cake mix and after cooking, blend 25 g unrefined icing sugar with about 1 tablespoon of freshly squeezed orange or lemon juice to form a thin icing. Drizzle over the tops of the bars once they have cooled.

NUTRITIONAL INFORMATION
Kcal: **158**
Fat: **5 g (0.6 g saturated)**
Protein: **4.6 g**
Carbohydrate: **24 g**

fruity carrot cake

This delicious, moist cake is packed full of fruits – from prunes and dried apricots to grated fresh apple.

100 ml sunflower oil

120 g light muscovado sugar

1 egg, beaten

3 egg whites

175 g carrots, peeled and coarsely grated

1 cooking apple, about 175 g, peeled, cored and grated

225 g sultanas

100 g prunes, chopped

50 g dried apricots, chopped

75 g dried blueberries or sour cherries

1 teaspoon ground cinnamon

1 teaspoon baking powder

300 g wholemeal stoneground plain flour

50 g self-raising flour

2 teaspoons demerara sugar

a deep cake tin, 20.5 cm diameter, greased and lined with parchment paper

Makes 12 slices

Preparation time: 15–20 minutes

Pour the oil into a large bowl, add the sugar and beat until smooth and free from lumps. Beat in the whole egg and the egg whites a little at a time. Add the carrot, apple and dried fruit and stir well.

Sift the cinnamon, baking powder and flours into the mixture, adding any bran left in the sieve to the bowl. Stir gently until incorporated. Do not overmix. Spoon the mixture into the prepared cake tin. Level the top with a spatula or round-bladed knife, then sprinkle the top with the demerara sugar.

Bake in a preheated oven at 170°C (325°F) Gas 3 for 1¼ hours, until cooked – a skewer inserted into the centre should come out clean. Remove from the oven and let cool in the tin before turning out. Store in an airtight container for up to 1 week.

NUTRITIONAL INFORMATION

Kcal: **296**
Fat: **9 g (1 g saturated)**
Protein: **6 g**
Carbohydrate: **50 g**

quick lunches and suppers

crispy toast and tomatoes

This is a really tasty suggestion for a quick breakfast, lunch or supper.

1 teaspoon olive oil

2 small leeks, thinly sliced

10 button mushrooms, about 50 g, sliced

4 slices wholegrain bread

30 g low-fat spread

200 g cherry tomatoes, halved

3 teaspoons finely chopped fresh basil leaves

2 teaspoons finely chopped fresh oregano

2 teaspoons finely chopped fresh flat leaf parsley

freshly ground black pepper

Serves 2

NUTRITIONAL INFORMATION
Kcal: **142**
Fat: **4.5 g (1.6 g saturated)**
Protein: **6 g**
Carbohydrate: **18 g**

Preparation time: 5–6 minutes

Heat the oil in a frying pan, add the leeks and mushrooms and cook over medium heat for 4–5 minutes, or until tender.

Meanwhile, toast the bread, then spread it very lightly with the low-fat spread.

Add the tomatoes and herbs to the leek mixture and cook for a further 1–2 minutes, or until heated through. Season with pepper. Serve the toast topped with the tomato and leek mixture.

Variation: This would make an ideal filling for warmed split pita bread. Add 1 thinly sliced and deseeded red or yellow pepper at the same time as the leeks, if you like. If you can buy some wild mushrooms, use them instead of the button ones for extra flavour.

full of beans soup

When the hunger pangs set in at lunchtime I make this soup. It's quick and easy to throw together, yet it tastes so rich and herby that you would be forgiven for thinking it was the result of a real labour of love.

750 g ripe tomatoes, halved

2 tablespoons chopped fresh basil leaves

2–3 garlic cloves, crushed

400 g canned mixed beans, drained and rinsed

100 g canned red kidney beans, drained and rinsed

1 vegetable stock cube

sea salt and freshly ground black pepper

To serve

half-fat crème fraîche (optional)

freshly grated Parmesan cheese

1 tablespoon chopped fresh basil leaves

Serves 4

Preparation time: 10 minutes

Put the tomatoes in a large roasting tin, cut sides up. Sprinkle with the basil and garlic, then season well with salt and pepper. Put under a preheated hot grill for 5–10 minutes, until the tomatoes have softened.

Remove the tomatoes from the grill and let cool slightly. When cool enough to handle, peel the tomatoes, discarding the skins. Put the tomatoes in a food processor or blender and process until smooth. Add the mixed beans and kidney beans and process for a further 30 seconds, until the beans are broken down slightly but the soup still has a chunky texture.

Transfer the mixture to a saucepan. Dissolve the stock cube in 150 ml of boiling water. Add the stock to the soup and heat gently over medium heat until piping hot, stirring occasionally.

Ladle the soup into warmed soup bowls. Serve immediately, topped with 1 dessertspoon of half-fat crème fraîche, if using, a sprinkling of freshly grated Parmesan and some chopped basil.

Variation: To make this soup even quicker, substitute the fresh tomatoes for 1 kg canned tomatoes. Don't forget to add plenty of fresh herbs. Use coriander instead of the basil, if you prefer.

> **NUTRITIONAL INFORMATION**
> Kcal: **172**
> Fat: **3 g (1.6 g saturated)**
> Protein: **10 g**
> Carbohydrate: **29 g**

prawn and mango salad

Prawns are an excellent source of vitamin B12, which is necessary for the formation of blood cells and nerves. Prawns also provide selenium, which can help to protect against heart disease and cancer. This salad is a really tasty, light supper and makes a great barbecue dish, too.

NUTRITIONAL INFORMATION
Kcal: **167**
Fat: **5.5 g (0.8 g saturated)**
Protein: **14 g**
Carbohydrate: **16.5 g**

20 large, uncooked tiger prawns

1 tablespoon sesame seeds

1 tablespoon chopped fresh coriander

Marinade

2.5 cm piece fresh ginger, peeled and grated

1–2 red chillies, deseeded and chopped

4 tablespoons freshly squeezed lime juice

1 tablespoon olive oil

2 tablespoons light soy sauce

½ teaspoon brown sugar

1–2 garlic cloves, crushed

Mango salad

100 g bok choy, shredded

1 large ripe mango, peeled, stoned and chopped

75 g beansprouts

½ medium cucumber, chopped

1 red pepper, deseeded and thinly sliced

1 bunch spring onions, trimmed and chopped

olive oil, for drizzling

freshly ground black pepper

Serves 4

Preparation time: 15 minutes

Peel the prawns and, if necessary, discard the thin black vein that runs down the back. Rinse and pat dry with kitchen paper. Put in a shallow dish.

To make the marinade, put the ginger, chillies, lime juice, oil, soy sauce, sugar and garlic in a bowl. Mix well. Pour the marinade over the prawns, stir, then cover. Refrigerate and let marinate for 15–30 minutes.

Meanwhile, prepare the salad. Put the bok choy and mango in a serving bowl. Add the beansprouts, cucumber, red pepper, spring onions and black pepper, to taste. Mix well and reserve.

Drain the prawns, reserving the marinade. Heat a non-stick frying pan or wok, add the prawns and cook, stirring frequently, for 2–3 minutes, or until pink. Add to the mango salad.

Pour the marinade into a small saucepan. Bring to the boil and boil for 2 minutes. Pour the marinade over the salad and toss lightly. Sprinkle with the sesame seeds and coriander and serve immediately.

Variation: Replace the tiger prawns with monkfish. Cut the monkfish away from the central bone and discard any skin. Cut into small pieces and marinate as above. Cook as above for 4–5 minutes. Add a few cooked peeled prawns to the monkfish for the last 2 minutes of cooking time, if you like.

salad niçoise

The beauty of basing your diet around the glycaemic index is that no food needs to be ruled out altogether. Potatoes, for example, tend to score quite high on the glycaemic index, especially when mashed (GI 70) or baked (GI 85). New potatoes, which are used in this recipe, have a GI rating of approximately 62. This is still fairly high but when eaten in small amounts and combined with a protein-rich food, such as tuna, the effect of the potatoes on the overall GI of the meal is considerably reduced.

Preparation time: 15 minutes

Bring a saucepan of lightly salted water to the boil, add the potatoes and cook for 10–15 minutes, or until just tender. Drain, set aside and cover to keep warm.

Cook the French beans in a saucepan of boiling water for 5–6 minutes, until just tender. Drain well, add to the potatoes, cover again to keep warm. Drain the anchovy fillets on kitchen paper, then soak in milk for 10 minutes to remove excess salt. Rinse, then chop coarsely.

Rinse the tuna steaks and pat dry on kitchen paper. Season on both sides with black pepper. Preheat a stove-top griddle pan, add the tuna and cook for 3–4 minutes on each side until cooked to personal preference. Try to keep it slightly pink in the middle, because it can become dry if overcooked.

Drain the tuna on kitchen paper and cut into bite-sized pieces. Add the tuna, tomatoes, anchovies, capers and olives to the potatoes and beans. Toss well, set aside and keep warm.

To make the dressing, put the oil, garlic, lemon juice and zest and basil leaves in a small saucepan. Heat over medium heat for 2–3 minutes. Mix and season with salt and pepper.

Put the tuna mixture in a warm serving dish, pour over the dressing and toss carefully. Sprinkle with fresh basil leaves, then serve on a bed of salad leaves, accompanied by some warm wholemeal pita bread, if using.

Variation: Replace the tuna with diced grilled chicken or turkey breast and add some chicory leaves. For a vegetarian alternative, use diced marinated feta cheese.

225 g baby new potatoes

300 g French beans, trimmed

8 anchovy fillets

4 tuna steaks, about 150 g each

115 g baby plum tomatoes, halved

2 tablespoons capers in brine, drained and rinsed

25 g pitted black olives in brine, drained and rinsed

fresh basil leaves (optional)

Dressing

1 tablespoon olive oil

1 garlic clove, crushed

1 tablespoon freshly squeezed lemon juice

½ teaspoon finely grated unwaxed lemon zest

1 tablespoon shredded fresh basil leaves

sea salt and freshly ground black pepper

To serve

salad leaves

warm wholemeal pita bread (optional)

Serves 4

NUTRITIONAL INFORMATION

Kcal: **301**
Fat: **9 g (2 g saturated)**
Protein: **30 g**
Carbohydrate: **9 g**

400 g canned chopped tomatoes

3 garlic cloves, crushed

1 tablespoon mild chilli powder, or to taste

a pinch of dried oregano

1 tablespoon tomato purée

1 tablespoon olive oil

1 yellow pepper, deseeded and sliced

1 green pepper, deseeded and sliced

400 g canned refried beans, or canned borlotti or pinto beans, rinsed, drained and mashed

4 large wheat tortillas, 20 cm diameter

100 g extra-mature Cheddar cheese, grated

4 tablespoons Salsa (see below)

2 tablespoons half-fat crème fraîche

2 tablespoons chopped fresh coriander

sea salt and freshly ground black pepper

Salsa

½ large red onion

2 tomatoes

½ green chilli, deseeded and finely chopped

1 tablespoon freshly squeezed lime juice

1 tablespoon chopped fresh mint

Serves 4

vegetable burritos

Wheat tortillas have a glycaemic index rating of about 30, which makes them an ideal basis for a low-GI meal. These burritos use refried beans, which also have a low GI and are high in fibre, and there are plenty of antioxidant-packed peppers and tomatoes. They make a perfect TV dinner or can be served as a mid-week supper for friends and family.

Put the tomatoes in a saucepan with the garlic, chilli powder, oregano and tomato purée. Bring to the boil, reduce the heat and simmer for 10 minutes, until the mixture reduces slightly and begins to thicken.

Meanwhile, heat the oil in a separate saucepan. Add the peppers and sauté for about 5 minutes, until soft. Add the peppers to the tomato mixture. Put the refried beans in a saucepan and heat gently, stirring frequently until piping hot.

Wrap the tortillas in foil and warm in a preheated oven at 200°C (400°F) Gas 6 for 6–7 minutes, until soft and piping hot. Or heat according to the instructions on the packet. Remove from the oven and put the tortillas on 4 serving plates. Spread each tortilla with a thick layer of beans, then 1 tablespoon of the tomato and pepper mixture, 25 g cheese, 1 tablespoon of salsa and ½ tablespoon of crème fraîche. Sprinkle with coriander, fold and serve immediately.

Variations: For a non-vegetarian alternative, add 50 g sliced grilled chicken breast to each tortilla.

NUTRITIONAL INFORMATION
Kcal: **401**
Fat: **12 g (5 g saturated)**
Protein: **20 g**
Carbohydrate: **56 g**

cheesy lentil hash

Lentils are a superfood. Not only do they score as low as 26 on the glycaemic index, making them particularly slow releasing and sustaining, but they are a good source of protein, fibre, potassium, zinc and folic acid. You can serve this as a side dish, as you would mashed potatoes, use it as a topping on a baked sweet potato or eat it just as it is.

1 vegetable stock cube

850–900 ml water

400 g red split lentils

1 tablespoon soy sauce

1 large onion, very finely chopped

2 celery sticks, very thinly sliced

2–3 garlic cloves, crushed

2 tablespoons tomato purée

100 g extra-mature Cheddar cheese, grated

a baking dish

Serves 4–6

Preparation time: 10 minutes

Dissolve the stock cube in 850 ml boiling water. Stir well. Put the stock in a saucepan and add the lentils. Bring to the boil, then reduce the heat and let simmer for 15–20 minutes, adding more water if necessary, until all the liquid is absorbed and the lentils are soft.

Meanwhile, heat the soy sauce and 4 tablespoons of water in a frying pan. Add the onions, celery and garlic and sauté for 8–10 minutes or until soft. Add the lentils and the tomato purée to the pan. Heat, stirring, until piping hot.

Transfer to a baking dish and sprinkle with the grated cheese. Heat under a preheated hot grill for about 2 minutes, until the cheese begins to melt. Serve immediately.

Variation: Mix in some chopped nuts or seeds of your choice to give some added bite. Alternatively, sprinkle with some chopped, grilled dry-cured bacon just before serving.

NUTRITIONAL INFORMATION
Kcal: **468**
Fat: **12 g (7 g saturated)**
Protein: **31 g**
Carbohydrate: **61 g**

baked sweet potato with mexican beans

If you are looking for a meal that will really fill you up, try this. Sweet potatoes make a nutritious, tasty, low-GI alternative to ordinary potatoes and the mixed beans help to lower the GI of the meal even further. The other great thing is that sweet potatoes are far more moist than other potatoes when baked so there is no need to add butter after cooking.

4 sweet potatoes, about 200 g each

1 tablespoon olive oil

1 onion, finely chopped

2 garlic cloves, crushed (optional)

2 red chillies, deseeded and finely chopped (optional)

2 tablespoons red wine vinegar

1 tablespoon Worcestershire sauce

600 g canned chopped tomatoes

400 g canned mixed beans, drained and rinsed

1 tablespoon fresh chopped coriander

50 g extra-mature Cheddar cheese, grated, to serve (optional)

Serves 4

Preparation time: 15–20 minutes

Scrub the potatoes and prick all over with a fork. Preheat the oven to 200°C (400°F) Gas 6 and cook the potatoes for 1–1¼ hours, or until soft. Alternatively, wrap the potatoes in kitchen paper and microwave each one on high for 3½–4 minutes, or until soft. Let the potatoes stand for 1 minute.

Heat the oil in a non-stick saucepan. Add the onion, garlic and chillies, if using, red wine vinegar and Worcestershire sauce. Sauté until the onions are soft, about 5 minutes. Add the tomatoes to the pan, bring to the boil, lower the heat and simmer for 10 minutes. Add the beans, stir and cook for a few minutes more until they are piping hot. Stir in the fresh coriander.

Cut the sweet potatoes in half. Put 2 halves on each serving plate and spoon the Mexican beans over the top. Sprinkle with some grated Cheddar cheese, if using, and serve immediately.

Variation: Peel the potatoes, cut them into chunks and cook in lightly salted water for 20 minutes, or until soft. Drain and mash, keeping the mixture fairly dry. Shape into 4–6 nests and put on a non-stick baking sheet.
Meanwhile, prepare the beans as above, then spoon the mixture into the nests. Sprinkle with the Cheddar cheese and bake as above for 20 minutes. Serve.

NUTRITIONAL INFORMATION
Kcal: **420**
Fat: **10 g (3 g saturated)**
Protein: **15 g**
Carbohydrate: **75 g**

rice and bean burgers

200 g brown rice
(not quick-cook variety)

2 tablespoons Worcestershire
sauce

1 onion, chopped

2 garlic cloves, crushed

200 g canned cannellini beans,
drained and rinsed

200 g canned red kidney beans,
drained and rinsed

50 g fresh stoneground
wholemeal breadcrumbs

1 egg, beaten

115 g grated mature Cheddar
cheese

2 tablespoons chopped
fresh thyme

1 small green pepper, deseeded
and chopped

1 large carrot, coarsely grated

wholemeal flour or cornmeal,
for coating

2–3 tablespoons sunflower oil

sea salt and freshly ground
black pepper

To serve

salad leaves

relish

a baking sheet

Makes 10–12

There's something really satisfying about making your own burgers, especially when the finished product is superior to anything you might find in the shops. This recipe takes a little longer than the others in this book but you will be rewarded with at least 5 meals (2 burgers per meal) for your labour. Simply pop any leftover burgers in the freezer before you cook them and take them out as and when you need them.

Preparation time: 30 minutes

Cook the rice according to the instructions on the packet, allowing it to slightly overcook so that it is soft. Drain the rice, transfer it to a large bowl and reserve. Put 2 tablespoons of water and 2 tablespoons of Worcestershire sauce in a frying pan, add the onion and garlic and cook over medium heat until softened, about 8 minutes.

Put the onions, garlic, cooked rice, beans, breadcrumbs, egg, cheese and thyme in a food processor or blender. Add plenty of salt and pepper, then process until combined. Add the green pepper and grated carrot and mix well. Put the mixture in the refrigerator and chill for 1½ hours, or until quite firm.

Shape the mixture into 10–12 burgers, using wet hands if the mixture sticks. Coat them in flour or cornmeal and chill for a further 30 minutes.

Put the burgers on a non-stick baking sheet and brush lightly with a little oil. Cook in a preheated oven at 190°C (375°F) Gas 5 for 20–25 minutes, or until piping hot. Alternatively, heat the oil in a non-stick frying pan and fry the burgers for 3–4 minutes on each side, or until piping hot. Serve immediately, accompanied by salad leaves and relish.

Variation: Add 1–2 deseeded finely chopped chillies to give an extra bite and 3 finely chopped celery sticks to add some crunch, if you like. Replace the thyme with chopped fresh coriander.

NUTRITIONAL INFORMATION
Kcal: **263**
Fat: **8 g (3 g saturated)**
Protein: **13 g**
Carbohydrate: **37 g**

pesto pasta

The pine nuts and olive oil traditionally used in pesto make it high in fat. The combination of garlic, fresh basil and half-fat crème fraîche used in this recipe creates a healthier, low-fat version while still packing a mean tasting punch!

150 ml fresh vegetable stock

175 g asparagus, trimmed and cut into 5 cm lengths

225 g mushrooms, wiped and sliced

300 g green and white tagliatelle

400 g canned artichoke hearts, drained and halved

150 g extra-lean ham, chopped

Pesto

4 garlic cloves, crushed

8 tablespoons chopped fresh basil leaves

8 tablespoons half-fat crème fraîche

4 tablespoons freshly grated Parmesan cheese

freshly ground black pepper

To serve

2 tablespoons shredded fresh basil leaves

fresh Parmesan cheese shavings

Serves 4

Preparation time: 12–15 minutes

Put the stock and asparagus in a saucepan. Bring to the boil, reduce the heat, cover and simmer for 2 minutes. Add the mushrooms and simmer for a further 2 minutes, until the asparagus is just tender. Drain and set aside.

Bring a large saucepan of lightly salted water to the boil. Add the pasta and cook until *al dente* – just tender, but still with a bite to it – or according to the timings on the packet.

Meanwhile, to make the pesto, put the garlic, basil, crème fraîche, Parmesan and black pepper in a food processor or blender. Process for a few seconds, until smooth. Alternatively, finely chop the basil and mix all the ingredients together in a bowl.

Drain the pasta and return it to the warm pan. Add the mushrooms, asparagus and artichokes to the pasta and cook over low heat stirring frequently for 2–3 minutes, until piping hot.

Remove the pan from the heat, add the pesto and ham and toss well. Serve immediately in warm bowls, sprinkled with shredded basil leaves and Parmesan shavings.

NUTRITIONAL INFORMATION
Kcal: **477**
Fat: **15 g (5 g saturated)**
Protein: **27 g**
Carbohydrate: **61 g**

creamy bacon and mushroom carbonara

The difference between this carbonara recipe and the more traditional version is that here we use skimmed milk instead of the usual egg yolks and cream, which are high in saturated fats. However, the white wine, extra-lean bacon and fresh herbs ensure there is no compromise on taste. Also, spaghetti is one of the lowest-GI pastas you can find.

250 g wholewheat spaghetti

8 slices extra-lean bacon, fat removed and thinly sliced

140 g small mushrooms, sliced

1 tablespoon olive oil

1 teaspoon wholegrain mustard

2 tablespoons white wine or vegetable stock

30 g grated extra-mature Cheddar cheese

3 teaspoons cornflour

250 ml skimmed milk

2 tablespoons chopped fresh flat leaf parsley

freshly ground black pepper

freshly grated Parmesan cheese, to serve (optional)

Serves 4

Preparation time: 10 minutes

Bring a large saucepan of lightly salted water to the boil. Add the spaghetti and cook until *al dente* – just tender, but still with a bite to it – or according to the timings on the packet.

Heat a non-stick frying pan, add the bacon and cook over high heat for 5 minutes, until browned, turning once. Add the mushrooms and oil to the pan and cook for 2 minutes. Stir in the mustard and wine or stock and cook for a further 3 minutes. Reduce the heat, add the grated Cheddar and stir until melted. Blend the cornflour with 2 tablespoons of water. Add to the pan and stir over low heat until the mixture becomes quite thick.

Remove the pan from the heat and let cool slightly. Season to taste with pepper, then gradually add the milk, stirring continuously until well combined. Do not heat the sauce at this stage or it may curdle. Stir in the parsley.

Drain the pasta and return it to the warm pan. Pour the carbonara sauce over the spaghetti and toss gently to mix. Divide between 4 bowls or plates and serve immediately, sprinkled with Parmesan cheese, if using.

Variation: Try using one grilled, sliced chicken breast instead of the bacon. For a vegetarian alternative, substitute some broccoli florets or peas for the bacon.

NUTRITIONAL INFORMATION
Kcal: **353**
Fat: **10 g (3 g saturated)**
Protein: **21 g**
Carbohydrate: **48 g**

chilli pasta bake

Fettuccine, with a GI rating of about 32, is one of the lowest-GI pastas available. It takes very little time to cook, which makes it the perfect ingredient for a quick evening meal.

225 g fettuccine

2 courgettes, chopped

2 leeks, chopped

2 garlic cloves, crushed

1–2 red chillies, deseeded and finely chopped

1 tablespoon chopped fresh oregano

1 tablespoon chopped fresh flat leaf parsley

600 ml passata

3 tablespoons half-fat crème fraîche

2 tablespoons freshly grated Parmesan cheese

sea salt and freshly ground black pepper

an ovenproof dish

Serves 4

Preparation time: 10–12 minutes

Bring a large saucepan of lightly salted water to the boil. Add the fettuccine and cook until *al dente* – just tender, but still with a bite to it – or according to the timings on the packet.

Heat a large non-stick saucepan, add the courgettes, leeks and garlic and dry fry for 2–3 minutes. Add the chillies, herbs, passata and crème fraîche. Drain the pasta and add to the chilli sauce. Season to taste with salt and pepper and stir well. Transfer to an ovenproof dish and sprinkle with the grated Parmesan.

Bake in a preheated oven at 190°C (375°F) Gas 5 for 30–35 minutes, until golden brown and bubbling. Serve immediately.

NUTRITIONAL INFORMATION
Kcal: **278**
Fat: **6 g (2 g saturated)**
Protein: **12.5 g**
Carbohydrate: **50 g**

prawn and butter bean rice

This makes a great mid-week supper dish. Feel free to increase your vegetable intake by adding vegetables of your choice. I like to throw in some frozen peas, corn kernels or green beans as I usually have them in my freezer, they cook in minutes and they don't require any preparation.

NUTRITIONAL INFORMATION
Kcal: **422**
Fat: **5 g (0.5 g saturated)**
Protein: **33 g**
Carbohydrate: **62 g**

Preparation time: 10 minutes

Heat the oil in a large non-stick saucepan. Add the rice, onion and turmeric and cook over medium heat, stirring, for 2 minutes. Add the tomatoes, pepper, garlic, stock and salt and pepper, to taste. Cover the pan with a tight-fitting lid, reduce the heat and simmer for 15 minutes, until most of the stock has been absorbed by the rice.

Add the butter beans, chillies and prawns to the rice mixture and stir through gently. Replace the lid and cook for a further 3 minutes, or until the stock is absorbed and the prawns are thoroughly warmed through. Stir in the coriander and serve immediately.

Variation: Brown four skinned, boneless chicken thighs in the oil then add to the rice and onion and proceed as above. Add some frozen peas and corn kernels with the butter beans and prawns and cook for 3–5 minutes or until cooked and piping hot. Serve with lemon wedges, if you like.

1 tablespoon olive oil

200 g basmati rice

1 large onion, chopped

1 teaspoon ground turmeric

400 g canned chopped tomatoes

1 large red pepper, deseeded and finely chopped

1–2 garlic cloves, chopped

500 ml chicken stock

400 g canned butter beans, drained and rinsed

1–2 red chillies, deseeded and finely sliced

500 g cooked peeled prawns, thawed if frozen

3 tablespoons fresh coriander, coarsely chopped

sea salt and freshly ground black pepper

Serves 4

asian salmon with rice noodles

Rice noodles have a GI rating of approximately 40. Combine them with a high-protein food such as salmon, which will lower the GI of the meal even further, and plenty of fresh vegetables and you have a delicious, easy low-GI meal. Rice noodles are available from larger supermarkets.

4 salmon cutlets, about 115 g each

2 teaspoons Chinese five spice powder

300 g rice vermicelli noodles

2 tablespoons light soy sauce

2 teaspoons clear honey

2.5 cm piece fresh ginger, peeled and grated

2 garlic cloves, crushed

1 large carrot, about 125 g, thinly sliced

1 large leek, about 150 g, sliced

350 g mushrooms, wiped and sliced

1 tablespoon chopped fresh coriander (optional)

freshly ground black pepper

Serves 4

Preparation time: 15 minutes

Wash the salmon cutlets and pat dry with kitchen paper. Rub the five spice powder into both sides of the fish and season well with black pepper. Set aside for 30 minutes.

Meanwhile, put the noodles in a bowl, cover with boiling water and let soak for 15 minutes. Drain, then add the noodles to a saucepan of boiling water and cook for 1 minute. Drain and keep the noodles warm.

Cook the salmon cutlets under a preheated hot grill for 7–10 minutes, or until thoroughly cooked, turning once halfway through the cooking time.

Heat a non-stick frying pan. Add the soy sauce, honey, ginger, garlic, carrot and leek to the pan and sauté the vegetables for 3–4 minutes, until beginning to soften. Add the mushrooms to the pan and sauté for a further 2 minutes.

Divide the noodles between 4 bowls or plates. Spoon the vegetables and their juices over the noodles and put the grilled salmon on top. Sprinkle with coriander, if using, and serve.

Variation: Replace the leeks with thinly sliced courgettes and add some sugar snap peas and tiny broccoli florets. If you like, try using oyster or fresh shiitake mushrooms and add some shredded Chinese cabbage leaves or bok choy.

NUTRITIONAL INFORMATION
Kcal: **580**
Fat: **14 g (3 g saturated)**
Protein: **32 g**
Carbohydrate: **72 g**

chargrilled salmon, spinach and tomato stack

This is one of the fastest, easiest and most delicious meals you could hope for. The salmon is a great source of essential fatty acids, which support brain function, strengthen the immune system and help prevent heart disease. So although this meal is a little higher in fat than most, don't worry – it's the right sort of fat. Just tuck in and enjoy.

Preparation time: 5 minutes

Lightly brush a stove-top grill pan with the olive oil and then heat until sizzling hot. Add the salmon to the pan, skin side down. Add the tomato and sprinkle with half the basil leaves. Cook for 3–4 minutes. Turn over the salmon and the tomato and cook for a further 2–3 minutes, until the salmon is cooked through but still tender. Remove the pan from the heat.

Put the spinach leaves on a serving plate, top with the tomato slice and then the salmon. Drizzle with a few drops of olive oil and some balsamic vinegar, then sprinkle with the remaining chopped basil leaves. Serve immediately.

1 tablespoon olive oil, plus extra to serve

1 salmon fillet, about 150 g, trimmed and boned

1 thick slice beef tomato

2 teaspoons finely chopped fresh basil leaves

a handful of spinach leaves, rinsed

1 tablespoon balsamic vinegar

Serves 1

NUTRITIONAL INFORMATION
Kcal: **427**
Fat: **25 g (5 g saturated)**
Protein: **38 g**
Carbohydrate: **2.5 g**

---

creamed leek and smoky fish pie

This is a favourite in my household. The combination of creamy crème fraîche and cheese with the smokiness of the fish and the slight crunchiness of the leeks makes every mouthful a delight.

Preparation time: 25 minutes

Lightly rinse the fish and put it in a large frying pan. Add the milk and bay leaves and slowly bring to the boil. Reduce the heat and let simmer for 5 minutes. Remove the pan from the heat, then transfer the fish to a baking dish using a slotted spoon. Let it cool slightly before flaking it into pieces.

Add the mushrooms, peas and corn kernels to the milk remaining in the frying pan and bring back to the boil. Reduce the heat and simmer gently for 5 minutes. Remove the vegetables from the milk with a slotted spoon and transfer them to the baking dish. Strain off 300 ml of the milk and reserve. Add the salmon strips to the baking dish.

Put the leeks in a clean frying pan with 8 tablespoons of water. Bring to the boil, reduce the heat and simmer for about 8 minutes, stirring occasionally, until softened. Remove the pan from the heat and let cool before stirring in the crème fraîche.

Blend the cornflour to a smooth paste with a little of the reserved milk. Put the remainder of the reserved milk in a saucepan and bring to the boil. Stir the paste into the boiling milk and cook, stirring, until thickened. Add the parsley and black pepper, to taste, then pour the sauce over the fish mixture and mix lightly.

Spoon the creamy leeks over the top of the fish to completely cover it. Sprinkle with the cheese, then bake in a preheated oven at 200°C (400°F) Gas 6 for 25–30 minutes, until bubbling.

Serve accompanied by lemon wedges and your choice of vegetables, such as the Spinach, Mangetout, Peas and Spring Onions (see right) or Tarragon Baby Carrots (see page 90).

Variation: If you prefer a less smoky fish flavour, replace half the smoked haddock with either fresh cod or haddock. Cook it with the smoked haddock, as above.

900 g smoked haddock or smoked cod fillets, skinned and bones removed

600 ml skimmed milk

2 bay leaves

115 g button mushrooms, quartered

115 g frozen peas

115 g frozen corn kernels

60 g smoked salmon, thinly sliced

600 g leeks, sliced

5 tablespoons half-fat crème fraîche

3 tablespoons cornflour

1–2 tablespoons chopped fresh flat leaf parsley

25 g extra-mature Cheddar cheese, grated

freshly ground black pepper

To serve

lemon wedges

vegetables

a large baking dish

Serves 4

NUTRITIONAL INFORMATION
Kcal: **543**
Fat: **14 g (5 g saturated)**
Protein: **68 g**
Carbohydrate: **41 g**

spinach, mangetout, peas and spring onions side dish

Research shows that one of the best ways to improve your health and protect yourself from getting cancer and heart disease is to increase your intake of fruit and vegetables. Current guidelines recommend a minimum of five servings of fruit and vegetables per day and the greater variety you can eat, the better. This side dish combines spinach, mangetout, peas and spring onions and is a great accompaniment to almost any meal.

20 g polyunsaturated margarine

5 spring onions, thinly sliced

80 ml white wine

200 g frozen peas

100 g mangetout

250 g spinach, rinsed, thoroughly drained and tough stalks removed

sea salt and freshly ground black pepper

Serves 4

Preparation time: 6 minutes

Heat a non-stick saucepan. Add the margarine, spring onions and 2 tablespoons of wine and sauté for 2 minutes. Add the peas and mangetout and cook for a further 2 minutes. Add the remaining wine, bring to the boil, reduce the heat, cover and simmer for 2 minutes. Add the spinach and cook for a further 30 seconds, until the spinach is just wilted. Season to taste with salt and pepper and serve immediately.

Variation: Replace the mangetout with small florets of broccoli, if you prefer.

NUTRITIONAL INFORMATION
Kcal: **91**
Fat: **3.5 g (0.7 g saturated)**
Protein: **5 g**
Carbohydrate: **7 g**

bag-baked chicken with butter beans

Whenever you have one of those days when you really don't feel like cooking, make this supper. Just put all the ingredients together in a bag then sit back and relax while it cooks.

10 baby leeks, washed

100 g baby carrots, halved

400 g canned butter beans, drained, rinsed and mashed

4 skinless, boneless chicken breasts

100 g baby corn

100 g French beans, trimmed

2–3 garlic cloves, sliced

fresh tarragon sprigs, plus extra chopped tarragon, to serve

120 ml white wine or chicken stock

1 teaspoon Dijon mustard

150 ml half-fat crème fraîche

sea salt and freshly ground black pepper

vegetables, to serve

a baking sheet

Serves 4

Preparation time: 15 minutes

Using wide foil, make a large parcel in which to cook the chicken. Cut 2 pieces of foil, each about 30 cm in length. Put the 2 pieces on top of each other, fold 3 sides in and leave 1 side open.

Bring a saucepan of water to the boil, add the leeks and carrots and cook for 2 minutes, until just beginning to soften. Drain and put in the foil bag. Add the mashed beans, chicken, baby corn, French beans, garlic, tarragon sprigs and white wine or stock. Season well with salt and pepper, then fold the foil over, pinching the edges together firmly. Carefully slide the parcel on to a baking sheet.

Bake in the middle of a preheated oven at 220°C (425°F) Gas 7 for 25 minutes, or until the chicken is cooked. Test by inserting a skewer into the thickest part, the juices should run clear, with no sign of blood.

Meanwhile, put the mustard and the crème fraîche in a bowl and mix.

Remove the parcel from the oven and open carefully. Transfer the contents to warm serving plates. Top with a spoonful of the crème fraîche mixture and sprinkle with fresh chopped tarragon. Serve immediately on its own or with your choice of vegetables, such as the Almond Broccoli (see right).

NUTRITIONAL INFORMATION
Kcal: **367**
Fat: **9 g (3 g saturated)**
Protein: **44 g**
Carbohydrate: **27 g**

almond broccoli side dish

This is a match made in heaven. Broccoli is rich in phytochemicals and vitamin C, which protect you from a whole host of diseases, including cancer. Make sure you steam the broccoli because boiling almost halves its vitamin C content. Almonds are another superfood. They are high in healthy, unsaturated, heart-protecting fats and are packed full of essential minerals, such as calcium, iron, zinc and magnesium.

450 g broccoli, divided into small florets

50 g flaked almonds, toasted

freshly squeezed juice of ½ lemon

Serves 4

Preparation time: 8 minutes

Steam the broccoli over a pan of boiling water for 5–8 minutes, until cooked but still slightly firm to the bite. Remove the pan from the heat.

Transfer the broccoli to a warm serving dish, sprinkle with the almonds and lemon juice and serve immediately.

Variation: Place whole blanched almonds on a baking sheet and cook in a preheated oven at 200°C (400°F) Gas 6 for 10–12 minutes, or until golden. Use instead of the toasted flaked almonds.

NUTRITIONAL INFORMATION
Kcal: 113
Fat: 7 g (0.8 g saturated)
Protein: 8 g
Carbohydrate: 3 g

tarragon baby carrots side dish

Fresh baby carrots taste delicious just as they are. But there is something about the hint of aniseed from the tarragon and the sharpness of the lemon juice that takes them to a whole new dimension.

350 g baby carrots

10 g polyunsaturated margarine

1 tablespoon freshly squeezed lemon juice

1 tablespoon finely chopped fresh tarragon

Serves 4

Preparation time: 8 minutes

Steam the carrots over boiling water for 5–8 minutes, or until they are cooked but still have some bite to them. Remove the pan from the heat and transfer the carrots to a warm serving dish. Top with the margarine, let it melt, then sprinkle with the lemon juice and tarragon. Toss gently and serve.

Variation: Replace the tarragon with chopped fresh coriander, and add 1 chopped garlic clove to the carrots while they are cooking.

NUTRITIONAL INFORMATION
Kcal: **37**
Fat: **2.5 g** (0.5 g saturated)
Protein: **1 g**
Carbohydrate: **3.5 g**

chicken and barley supper

2 tablespoons wholemeal flour

500 g skinless, boneless chicken breasts, cut into cubes

100 g lean bacon slices, cut into strips

2 medium onions, chopped

2 carrots, sliced

2 celery sticks, chopped

750–900 ml white wine or chicken stock

3 tablespoons pearl barley, rinsed

1 tablespoon mixed chopped fresh herbs, such as rosemary, basil, parsley and thyme

freshly ground black pepper

To serve

chopped fresh parsley

vegetables

Serves 4

Preparation time: 15 minutes

Season the flour with black pepper, then toss the chicken cubes in the flour. Heat a large non-stick frying pan or saucepan, add the bacon and dry fry for 5 minutes, stirring frequently, until the fat starts to run. Add the chicken and sauté for 5–8 minutes, turning frequently, until the chicken is sealed all over. Remove the chicken and bacon from the pan with a slotted spoon and set aside.

Add the onion, carrots, celery and 4 tablespoons of the wine or stock to the pan and sauté for 5 minutes, until the vegetables are softened. Add the pearl barley, herbs and 600 ml of the wine or stock. Bring to the boil, then cover, reduce the heat and simmer for 1 hour. Add more wine or stock as it is absorbed.

Return the chicken and bacon to the pan and continue to simmer for a further 30 minutes, or until the pearl barley and chicken are tender. Stir occasionally during cooking, adding a little more wine or stock, if necessary. Serve, sprinkled with chopped parsley and accompanied by a selection of your favourite vegetables, such as the Tarragon Baby Carrots (see left).

Variation: Use half the amount of chicken and cook as above. Once all the ingredients are tender, use a slotted spoon to remove 2–3 tablespoons of the mixture and reserve. Put the remainder in a food processor and blend to form a purée. Return to a clean saucepan together with the reserved ingredients. Heat until piping hot, adding a little extra stock or water to make a warming winter soup. You could do the same with any leftovers, taking care when reheating to make sure that it is piping hot.

NUTRITIONAL INFORMATION

Kcal: 431

Fat: 7 g (2 g saturated)

Protein: 55 g

Carbohydrate: 29 g

beef and tomato gratin

Protein-rich foods, such as meat, fish and poultry, naturally lower the overall GI of a meal. The GI of this dish is kept low by a combination of the minced beef and the courgettes and tomatoes that are used as a topping instead of the usual high-GI mashed potatoes. The minced beef is also an excellent source of iron, so this meal really will do wonders for flagging energy levels.

NUTRITIONAL INFORMATION
Kcal: **315**
Fat: **9 g (3.5 g saturated)**
Protein: **33 g**
Carbohydrate: **23 g**

Preparation time: 15–20 minutes

Put the milk, the whole onion, carrot, bay leaves and cloves in a small saucepan and slowly bring to the boil. Remove the pan from the heat, cover and let infuse for 30 minutes. Strain, reserving the milk.

In a large saucepan, dry fry the beef and onion for 4–5 minutes, until browned. Drain off any fat from the beef. Sprinkle the flour over the meat and cook, stirring, for 2 minutes. Gradually stir in the stock. Blend the tomato purée with 2 tablespoons of water or extra stock and add to the meat. Stir well. Add the mixed herbs and season to taste with salt and pepper. Bring to the boil, reduce the heat and simmer, covered, for 30 minutes, stirring occasionally.

Meanwhile, blanch the courgettes in boiling water for 2 minutes, then drain thoroughly. Transfer the beef mixture to a baking dish. Top with the courgettes, then cover with the sliced tomatoes.

Blend the cornflour to a smooth paste with a little of the infused milk. Bring the remainder of the milk to the boil. Stir the paste into the boiling milk and cook, stirring, until smooth and thickened. Cook, stirring, for a further 2 minutes. Add the ground mace or nutmeg and season to taste with salt and pepper.

Pour the sauce over the tomatoes and sprinkle with the Parmesan cheese. Put the baking dish on a baking sheet and bake in a preheated oven at 190°C (375°F) Gas 5 for 30–40 minutes, until golden brown. Sprinkle with the chopped parsley and serve.

300 ml skimmed milk

1 small onion

1 small carrot

2 bay leaves

3 whole cloves

340 g lean steak mince

1 large onion, finely chopped

2 tablespoons wholemeal flour

300 ml beef stock

1 tablespoon tomato purée

1 teaspoon dried mixed herbs

300 g courgettes, thinly sliced

2 large tomatoes, thinly sliced

2 tablespoons cornflour

$1/4$ teaspoon ground mace or freshly grated nutmeg

4 tablespoons freshly grated Parmesan cheese

sea salt and freshly ground black pepper

1 tablespoon chopped fresh flat leaf parsley, to serve

a large baking dish

Serves 4

entertaining

parma-wrapped asparagus

This starter, served with a light, crisp, well-chilled white wine, will get any dinner party off to a flying start. Not only does this look and taste delicious, but it is really easy to prepare. It can be made well in advance, leaving you more time to concentrate on your guests.

Preparation time: 12–15 minutes

Half-fill a saucepan with water and bring to the boil. Drop in the asparagus spears and cook for 1 minute. Drain the asparagus, plunge into cold water, then drain again.

Take 4 asparagus spears and 1 sprig of rosemary and wrap tightly in 1 slice of Parma ham. Make three more bundles in the same way. Put the asparagus bundles, cherry tomatoes and half the lemon wedges in a small roasting tin. Drizzle with the oil, then roast in a preheated oven at 220°C (425°F) Gas 7 for 5 minutes.

To serve, put 1 handful of rocket leaves on each of 4 serving plates. Add 1 asparagus bundle, 6 tomato halves and 1 lemon wedge to each plate. Squeeze the juice of the remaining lemon over the top, drizzle lightly with balsamic vinegar and sprinkle with a few shavings of Parmesan and some black pepper. Serve immediately.

Variations: Replace the Parma ham with lean dry-cured smoky bacon slices or thinly sliced smoked salmon.

16 asparagus spears, trimmed

4 sprigs fresh rosemary

4 slices Parma ham, fat removed

12 ripe cherry tomatoes, halved

2 lemons, 1 cut into wedges

1 teaspoon olive oil

1 tablespoon balsamic vinegar

1 tablespoon fresh Parmesan cheese shavings

freshly ground black pepper

4 handfuls rocket leaves, to serve

Serves 4

NUTRITIONAL INFORMATION
Kcal: **90**
Fat: **3.5 g (1.5 g saturated)**
Protein: **10 g**
Carbohydrate: **3 g**

tomato and basil bruschetta

No starter section would be complete without a recipe for bruschetta. Here are two of my all-time favourites.

4 thick slices stoneground wholemeal bread

1 tablespoon Dijon mustard

4 slices Parma ham

4 medium plum tomatoes, thickly sliced

1 tablespoon fresh shredded basil leaves

fresh Parmesan cheese shavings

sea salt and freshly ground black pepper

Serves 4

Preparation time: 5 minutes

Preheat the grill and line the grill tray with foil. Lightly toast the bread on both sides, then spread the slices with the mustard. Put 1 slice of Parma ham on top of each slice of bread. Top with the tomato slices, season with salt and pepper and sprinkle with basil.

Put under the hot grill for 2–3 minutes, until the tomatoes are just beginning to char. Remove from the grill, sprinkle with shavings of Parmesan, cut in half, if liked, and serve immediately.

Variation: Omit the Parma ham and top the tomatoes with some sautéed wild mushrooms and drained canned, sliced artichoke hearts. Sprinkle with some grated Parmesan cheese and cook under a preheated grill for 2–3 minutes, or until the cheese begins to melt. Serve immediately.

NUTRITIONAL INFORMATION
Kcal: **162**
Fat: **4.5 g (1.5 g saturated)**
Protein: **10.5 g**
Carbohydrate: **21 g**

charred vegetable bruschetta

2 teaspoons olive oil

1 onion, cut into wedges

2–3 garlic cloves, peeled and sliced

1 red pepper, deseeded and sliced

1 yellow pepper, deseeded and sliced

1 courgette, sliced

4 thick slices stoneground wholemeal bread

1 tablespoon tapenade

sea salt and freshly ground black pepper

To serve

fresh Parmesan cheese shavings

1 handful pitted black olives, such as Kalamata

fresh basil leaves

Serves 4

Preparation time: 5–6 minutes

Heat a non-stick frying pan. Add the oil, onion, garlic, peppers and courgette to the pan and sauté, stirring frequently, for 12–15 minutes, until the vegetables are beginning to char. Season to taste with salt and pepper.

Meanwhile, preheat the grill and line the grill tray with foil. Lightly toast the bread on both sides, then spread the 4 slices with the tapenade. Top with the charred vegetables. Serve immediately, sprinkled with shavings of Parmesan, olives and basil leaves.

Variation: Top the toasted bread with thin slices of dolcelatte cheese and put under a preheated grill. Cook for 2–3 minutes, until the cheese begins to melt. Remove from the grill and top with some sliced fresh figs and some fresh shredded mint leaves.

NUTRITIONAL INFORMATION
Kcal: **161**
Fat: **4 g (1.5 g saturated)**
Protein: **8 g**
Carbohydrate: **25 g**

sweet pear and stilton melt

Few starters are easier to make than this but it works wonderfully, both visually and on the taste buds. Because you are only using a small amount of Stilton, the overall fat content remains low, too.

NUTRITIONAL INFORMATION
Kcal: **222**
Fat: **7 g (1.7 g saturated)**
Protein: **3.5 g**
Carbohydrate: **27 g**

Preparation time: 4 minutes

4 firm, ripe pears, halved lengthways and cored

2 tablespoons freshly squeezed orange juice

70 g Stilton cheese, crumbled

1 tablespoon dried cranberries or sultanas

1 tablespoon toasted chopped hazelnuts

2 teaspoons finely grated unwaxed orange zest

1 tablespoon extra virgin olive oil

4 handfuls of bitter salad leaves

sea salt and freshly ground black pepper

Serves 4

Brush the pear halves with a little orange juice. Put the Stilton in a bowl and beat with a wooden spoon until creamy. Stir in the cranberries or sultanas, hazelnuts, orange zest and enough orange juice to moisten. Fill the pear hollows with the cheese mixture.

Preheat the grill to medium hot and line the grill tray with foil. Transfer the pears to the grill tray and grill for 3–4 minutes, until the cheese just begins to melt. Remove from the heat.

Put the olive oil, remaining orange juice and salt and pepper, to taste, in a large bowl. Beat well. Add the salad leaves and toss to coat. Divide the salad leaves between 4 serving plates. Put 2 pear halves on each plate and serve immediately.

Variation: Leave the pears whole. Core them with an apple corer and brush with lemon juice to prevent discolouration. Make the filling as above and use to stuff the pears, filling from the base. Chill for at least 30 minutes then serve on the dressed salad leaves.

hoummus

This dip isn't that low in fat, but it's lower than most conventional or shop-bought hoummus. If eaten in small amounts with plenty of vegetable crudités, it will do you the world of good!

Preparation time: 5 minutes

Put the garlic, chickpeas and 1 tablespoon of water in a food processor or blender and process for 1 minute. Add the tahini paste and process again for a further 1 minute, scraping down the sides after 30 seconds. Add the crème fraîche and ground cumin and process again. With the motor still running, slowly pour in the lemon juice and then sufficient water to give a soft consistency. Season to taste with salt and cayenne pepper and process once more.

Transfer the hoummus to a serving dish and sprinkle with the coriander. Serve with warm pita wedges and your choice of vegetable crudités. Alternatively, use the hoummus in sandwiches instead of butter.

NUTRITIONAL INFORMATION
Kcal: **206**
Fat: **14 g (2 g saturated)**
Protein: **9 g**
Carbohydrate: **11 g**

2 garlic cloves

400 g canned chickpeas, drained and rinsed

1 tablespoon tahini paste

4 tablespoons half-fat crème fraîche

1 teaspoon ground cumin

freshly squeezed juice of ½ lemon

cayenne pepper, to taste

2 teaspoons chopped fresh coriander

sea salt

To serve

warm pita bread, cut into wedges

selection of vegetable crudités, such as carrots, cucumber, radishes

Serves 6

baked mushrooms

Baked mushrooms often come swimming in oil in order to bring out their flavour. This can leave you feeling overloaded before you even get to the main course. This recipe, however, uses garlic, chillies and chives to give lots of flavour, so the fat content can remain low.

Preparation time 15 minutes

Choose 4 portabello or 8 chestnut mushrooms and remove the stalks. Put the caps stem side up in an ovenproof dish. Finely chop the remaining mushrooms and all the stalks. Heat a non-stick frying pan and add 2 teaspoons of the oil. Add the chopped mushrooms, celery, garlic and chilli and sauté, stirring frequently, until soft. Let cool slightly, then transfer to a bowl.

Add the breadcrumbs, tomato and chives to the bowl, then season to taste with salt and pepper. Mix well, adding a little oil to moisten, if necessary. Fill the mushrooms with the breadcrumb mixture. Pour about 4 tablespoons of water into the dish, then cook in a preheated oven at 180°C (350°F) Gas 4 for 12–15 minutes, until the mushrooms are soft and the topping is crisp. Remove from the oven and serve immediately, sprinkled with some chives and accompanied by mixed salad leaves.

Variation: For a really quick version, prepare the mushrooms as above. Put the remaining mushrooms with 2 garlic cloves, 50 g wholegrain bread, 6 spring onions, 50 g dried apricots, 25 g pecans and 2 tablespoons of fresh coriander in a food processor. Add salt and pepper, to taste. Process, adding a little lemon juice if necessary, to give a moist stuffing. Fill the mushrooms with this mixture and cook as above.

250 g medium chestnut or portabello mushrooms, wiped

2–4 teaspoons extra virgin olive oil

1 stick celery, finely chopped

1–2 large garlic cloves, crushed

1 green chilli, deseeded and finely chopped

50 g fresh wholegrain breadcrumbs

1 medium tomato, deseeded and chopped

2 tablespoons freshly snipped chives

sea salt and freshly ground black pepper

To serve

chives

mixed salad leaves

an ovenproof dish

Serves 4

NUTRITIONAL INFORMATION
Kcal: **80**
Fat: **3 g (0 g saturated)**
Protein: **3 g**
Carbohydrate: **10 g**

---

potted smoked trout

I always like a starter that can be made well in advance so I don't have to spend any time fussing over it when guests arrive. This recipe fits the bill perfectly.

125 g smoked trout fillets

1–2 tablespoons Dijon mustard

150 g low-fat cream cheese

1 tablespoon chopped fresh flat leaf parsley

sea salt and freshly ground black pepper

To serve

1 bunch watercress

wholemeal pita bread, grilled (optional)

4 ramekins, 150 ml each

Serves 4

Preparation time: 5 minutes

Put the trout fillets in a small bowl and flake with a fork. Add the mustard, Quark and parsley. Season to taste with salt and pepper and mix well. Press the mixture into the ramekins and smooth the tops with a round-bladed knife.

Refrigerate until ready to serve. Serve with watercress and strips of warm wholemeal pita, if liked.

NUTRITIONAL INFORMATION
Kcal: **74**
Fat: **2.5 g (0.5 g saturated)**
Protein: **10 g**
Carbohydrate: **2.5 g**

feta-stuffed peppers

Bulgur wheat is quick and easy to use, really versatile and the fact that the grains are whole makes it low GI (GI 48), too. This combination of bulgur wheat, sharp feta and sweet peppers tastes delicious and if you are really short on time you don't even need to cook them (see variation).

Preparation time: 12 minutes

100 g bulgur wheat

2 yellow peppers

2 orange peppers

1 red apple, such as Braeburn, cored and chopped

1 tablespoon freshly squeezed lemon juice

150 g feta cheese, crumbled

3 tablespoons mixed fresh herbs, such as dill, basil, parsley, mint and coriander

2 garlic cloves, crushed

3 cm piece fresh ginger, peeled and finely grated

50 g raisins

8 spring onions, finely chopped

1–2 tablespoons olive oil

sea salt and freshly ground black pepper

To serve (optional)

crisp green salad

wholemeal pita bread, grilled

a large ovenproof dish

Serves 4

Put the bulgur wheat in a bowl, cover with boiling water and let stand for 30 minutes, until the grains are puffed and swollen. Drain, if necessary, and fluff with a fork to separate the grains.

Meanwhile, cut the peppers in half lengthways and scrape out and discard the seeds and membranes. Leave the stalks intact so the peppers hold their shape. Transfer the peppers to an ovenproof dish.

Put the apple and lemon juice in a bowl and mix lightly. Add the drained bulgur wheat, feta, herbs, garlic, ginger, raisins, spring onions and oil. Season with salt and pepper and mix well.

Divide the bulgur wheat mixture between the halved peppers. Pour a small amount of water in the dish around the peppers and cook in a preheated oven at 180°C (350°F) Gas 4 for 20–25 minutes, until the filling is piping hot. Serve immediately, with a crisp, green salad and grilled wholemeal pita bread, if using.

Variation: This is an ideal recipe for families that have to cater for meat eaters and vegetarians. For meat eaters, replace the feta cheese with, or just add, some chopped cooked meat, such as ham or smoked turkey breast, or flaked smoked trout fillets. If you are really short on time, just fill the peppers with the bulgur wheat mixture and serve without cooking the peppers at all.

NUTRITIONAL INFORMATION
Kcal: **165**
Fat: **5 g (2 g saturated)**
Protein: **54 g**
Carbohydrate: **21 g**

chilli scallops with spaghetti

If you have friends coming round for a mid-week supper and you need to make something special but don't want to spend more than 10 minutes in the kitchen, this recipe is the answer. Spaghetti is a fairly low-GI pasta and the protein in the scallops, plus a little fat from the cream, help to keep the overall GI of the meal low, too.

Preparation time: 7–9 minutes

Rinse the scallops in cold water and discard the black vein, if necessary. Pat dry on kitchen paper. If the scallops are large, cut them into 2 or 3 slices.

Bring a large saucepan of water to the boil. Add a pinch of salt, then the spaghetti, and cook until *al dente* – just tender, but still with a bite to it – or according to the timings on the packet. Drain the pasta, reserving 2 tablespoons of the cooking water. Return the pasta and the reserved cooking water to the warm pan and reserve.

Put the garlic, chillies and coriander in a small bowl and mix. Heat a heavy-based frying pan and add 1 tablespoon of the oil. Add the chilli mixture to the pan and cook for 1 minute, stirring, then add the scallops. Stir well until coated with the oil and chillies. Cook, stirring occasionally, for 2–3 minutes, until the scallops are cooked. Season to taste with salt and pepper. Keep them warm in a low oven.

Add the cream and remaining oil to the spaghetti and heat gently, stirring frequently, until piping hot. Serve immediately, topped with the scallops.

Variation: Any seafood or shellfish, such as baby squid, would work well with this recipe. To prepare squid, rinse in cold water, discard the quill, remove the tentacles and trim. Slice the squid if large, but leave whole if small. Cook as above for 2–3 minutes, or until cooked. Serve as for the main recipe.

16–24 scallops

500 g spaghetti

4 garlic cloves, coarsely chopped

1–2 red chillies, deseeded and coarsely chopped

1 tablespoon chopped fresh coriander

2 tablespoons extra virgin olive oil

120 ml half-fat single cream

sea salt and freshly ground black pepper

Serves 4

NUTRITIONAL INFORMATION
Kcal: **585**
Fat: **11 g (4 g saturated)**
Protein: **39 g**
Carbohydrate: **112 g**

pan-fried salmon with cannellini bean purée

Who says you have to eat salmon with rice, potatoes or pasta? This novel, tasty and rather sophisticated recipe uses low-GI, high-fibre beans instead.

Preparation time: 10–12 minutes

Reserve a few rocket leaves for serving then put the remaining rocket, spinach and watercress in a salad bowl. Add the cherry tomatoes and set aside.

To make the cannellini bean purée, put the beans, garlic, lemon juice, thyme, oil and 2 tablespoons of water in a food processor or blender. Season with salt and pepper, to taste, then process to a smooth, soft purée. Add a little more water, if necessary. Transfer to a saucepan and heat gently for about 5 minutes, stirring frequently, until piping hot. Alternatively, put the purée in a microwaveable bowl, cover and cook on high for about 4 minutes, stirring halfway through, until piping hot. Let stand for 1 minute before serving.

Meanwhile, to cook the salmon fillets, heat the oil in a non-stick frying pan. Add the garlic and fry gently for 1 minute. Add the salmon and cook for 5–8 minutes, turning once halfway through.

Drizzle the salad with a little balsamic vinegar, season to taste with salt and pepper and toss well. Put a spoonful of cannellini bean purée on each of 4 warmed serving plates. Put the reserved rocket leaves on top, followed by the salmon. Drizzle with a little extra virgin olive oil. Serve immediately with the salad.

Variation: The bean purée would be delicious with most grilled foods. Try chicken, turkey, large prawns or tuna. Use other beans or a mixture of two or three types and keep the purée slightly chunky, if you prefer.

75 g rocket leaves

100 g baby spinach leaves, lightly rinsed

50 g watercress

16 cherry tomatoes, halved

4 salmon fillets, about 200 g each, trimmed and boned

1 tablespoon olive oil

4 cloves garlic, halved

balsamic vinegar, for drizzling

sea salt and freshly ground black pepper

Cannellini bean purée

400 g canned cannellini beans, drained and rinsed

1 garlic clove, crushed

1½ tablespoons freshly squeezed lemon juice

2 tablespoons chopped fresh thyme

2 teaspoons olive oil

sea salt and freshly ground black pepper

Serves 4

NUTRITIONAL INFORMATION
Kcal: **425**
Fat: **15 g (2 g saturated)**
Protein: **40 g**
Carbohydrate: **12.5 g**

NUTRITIONAL INFORMATION
Kcal: **425**
Fat: **11 g (1.5 g saturated)**
Protein: **41 g**
Carbohydrate: **44 g**

spicy tuna steaks with pepper noodles

Fresh tuna, unlike canned tuna, is a good source of those all-important omega-3 fatty acids, which help to protect against heart disease. Don't overcook the tuna because it can become quite dry and chewy. Fresh tuna is at its most tender when it is still pink in the middle.

4 tuna steaks, 175g each

2–3 garlic cloves, crushed

1 teaspoon ground cumin

2 teaspoons finely grated unwaxed lime zest

1 tablespoon freshly squeezed lime juice

2 teaspoons olive oil

1 teaspoon ground coriander

freshly ground black pepper

Pepper noodles

225 g egg noodles

1 teaspoon sunflower oil

1 garlic clove, chopped

1 red pepper, deseeded and thinly sliced

1 yellow pepper, deseeded and thinly sliced

finely grated zest and juice of 1 unwaxed lime

1 tablespoon light soy sauce

sea salt and freshly ground black pepper

To serve

1 red pepper, chopped

2 tablespoons chopped fresh coriander

4 lime wedges

Serves 4

Preparation time: 15 minutes

Wipe the tuna or lightly rinse and pat dry with kitchen paper. Put the garlic, cumin, lime zest, lime juice, oil, ground coriander and black pepper in a small bowl. Mix to make a paste. Spread the paste thinly on both sides of the tuna steaks and leave to marinate for at least 15 minutes.

Heat a non-stick frying pan until hot and press the tuna steaks into the pan to seal them. Lower the heat and cook for 3 minutes. Turn the fish over and cook for a further 3–5 minutes, until cooked to personal preference. Remove from the pan, transfer to a plate and keep warm in a low oven.

To make the pepper noodles, bring a large saucepan of water to the boil. Add the noodles and cook for 4 minutes, or according to the timings on the packet. Drain, rinse and reserve. Heat a non-stick frying pan, add the oil, garlic and peppers and sauté gently, until the vegetables start to soften. Add the drained noodles, the lime zest and juice and soy sauce. Cook for 1–2 minutes, turning frequently, until warmed through.

Transfer the noodles to warm serving plates and top with the tuna steaks. Sprinkle with some chopped red pepper and coriander. Add a wedge of lime and serve immediately.

Variation: Try a different marinade for the tuna: blend 2 crushed garlic cloves with 1 deseeded and finely chopped chilli, 2 teaspoons of freshly grated root ginger, 2 tablespoons of chopped fresh coriander, 1 teaspoon of Thai fish sauce and 1 tablespoon of olive oil. Marinate as above. Serve the tuna steaks on the Cannellini Bean Purée (page 106) or the Sweet Potato and Garlic Mash (page 113) instead of the noodles, if you prefer.

thai green chicken curry

Thai green curry is a really popular dish so it makes an ideal choice for a dinner party. The use of low-GI basmati rice and the addition of plenty of protein from the chicken helps to keep the overall GI of this meal low.

Preparation time: 10 minutes

Heat the oil in a large, heavy-based frying pan or wok. Add the onion and chillies and cook gently over medium heat for 5 minutes. Add the curry paste to the pan and cook, stirring frequently, for 2 minutes. Add the lemongrass and chicken and cook, stirring frequently, for a further 5 minutes, until the chicken is sealed.

Add the stock and coconut milk and bring to the boil. Reduce the heat and simmer gently for 15–20 minutes, until the chicken is tender.

To cook the rice, bring a large saucepan of water to the boil. Add the rice and return the water to the boil. Stir, then reduce the heat and simmer for 11 minutes. Drain and let stand for 2 minutes.

Meanwhile, bring a separate saucepan of water to the boil. Add the green beans and cook for 6–8 minutes, until just tender, then drain. Remove the lemongrass from the curry and stir in the beans and most of the coriander. Serve the curry on a bed of rice, sprinkled with the remaining coriander.

Variation: This curry would work equally well with fresh fish or shellfish instead of the chicken. You could use salmon, monkfish or large raw prawns, peeled if preferred, or a mixture of fish and shellfish. Adjust cooking times accordingly.

1 tablespoon olive oil

1 large onion, finely chopped

2 green chillies, deseeded and thinly sliced

2–3 tablespoons Thai green curry paste, to taste

1 stalk lemongrass, crushed

600 g chicken breasts or thigh fillets, fat removed and thinly sliced

450 ml hot chicken stock

150 ml low-fat coconut milk

400 g basmati rice

250 g green beans, diagonally sliced

2–3 tablespoons chopped fresh coriander

Serves 4

NUTRITIONAL INFORMATION
Kcal: **775**
Fat: **20 g (3 g saturated)**
Protein: **56 g**
Carbohydrate: **82 g**

stilton steaks with sweet potato and garlic mash

This dish is absolutely delicious, a real winner for either an informal dinner party or just a mid-week supper. The use of sweet potato for the mash instead of ordinary potatoes, coupled with the high-protein steaks, helps to keep the GI of the meal low.

Preparation time: 10 minutes

Bring a large saucepan of lightly salted water to the boil. Add the sweet potatoes, potatoes and garlic. Cook until tender, about 20 minutes.

Cook the steaks under a preheated hot grill for 8–10 minutes, depending on personal preference, turning once halfway through the cooking time. Divide the Stilton into 4 equal pieces and crumble over the top of the steaks a couple of minutes before removing them from the grill. Keep them warm in a low oven.

Drain the potatoes, reserving 60 ml of the cooking water. Return the potatoes and garlic to the warm saucepan. Add the oil and most of the oregano and season with salt and pepper. Mash well, adding a little of the reserved cooking water to moisten, if necessary.

Divide the mash between 4 warm serving plates and put the Stilton steaks on top. Sprinkle with some oregano leaves and serve immediately.

Variation: When in season, replace the potatoes with the equivalent weight of peeled Jerusalem artichokes.

600 g sweet potatoes, peeled and cut into chunks

200 g potatoes, peeled and cut into chunks

2–3 garlic cloves

4 sirloin steaks, about 225 g each

70 g Stilton cheese

1 tablespoon olive oil

6 sprigs fresh oregano, chopped

sea salt and freshly ground black pepper

Serves 4

NUTRITIONAL INFORMATION
Kcal: **571**
Fat: **18 g (6 g saturated)**
Protein: **54 g**
Carbohydrate: **54 g**

puddings

summer pudding

Summer berries are packed full of vitamin C, which helps to strengthen the immune system and fight infections. Now that frozen summer fruits are readily available in most supermarkets, you can enjoy this dessert all year round.

NUTRITIONAL INFORMATION
Kcal: **267**
Fat: **2 g (0.5 g saturated)**
Protein: **7 g**
Carbohydrate: **53 g**

Preparation time: 15 minutes

If you are using fresh fruit, lightly rinse and let dry. Put the berries, honey, red wine, water and cinnamon stick in a medium saucepan and gently simmer over low heat for 5 minutes, until the berries are plump and slightly softened. Remove from the heat and let cool. Discard the cinnamon stick.

Cut 6 slices of bread into triangles and use them to line the base and sides of the bowl or mould. Overlap the bread so it completely covers the bowl, leaving no gaps. Reserve the remaining 2 slices of bread to cover the top of the pudding. Spoon a little of the berry juice evenly over the bread in the bowl to moisten it. Fill the bowl with the berries, using a slotted spoon. Pack the fruit down with the back of a spoon, taking care not to squash the fruit too much. Cut the remaining 2 slices of bread into triangles. Put these on top of the fruit to make a lid. Reserve any remaining berry juice.

Cover the bowl with cling film, put a small plate or saucer on top, then put weights on the plate to press it down onto the pudding. Leave in the refrigerator overnight.

Remove the weights, plate and cling film. Put a large plate upside down on top of the bowl. Carefully invert the bowl and plate, then gently remove the bowl.

Put the reserved juice in a saucepan and heat gently. If necessary, gently drizzle the sauce over any parts of the pudding that are not a consistent colour. Blend the arrowroot, if using, with 1 tablespoon of water and stir into the hot juice. Keep stirring until the juice thickens and clears. Pour the sauce over the pudding. Serve with some low-fat yoghurt or crème fraîche and mint sprigs, if using.

500 g fresh or frozen berries, such as raspberries, blackberries, mulberries or mixed summer berries, thawed, if frozen

2 tablespoons clear honey

125 ml red wine

125 ml water

1 cinnamon stick, bruised

8 slices multi-grain day-old bread, crusts removed

1 teaspoon arrowroot (optional)

To serve (optional)

4 tablespoons low-fat yoghurt or half-fat crème fraîche

mint sprigs

a 475 ml bowl or mould

Serves 4

oaty plum crumbles

Plums, like cherries, apples and pears, are a particularly low-GI fruit. The crumble topping is made with jumbo oats, which helps to keep the GI of the overall dessert low, too.

750 g ripe plums, stoned and sliced

4 tablespoons water

1–2 tablespoons light muscovado sugar

half-fat crème fraîche, low-fat custard or ice cream, to serve

Crumble topping

100 g wholemeal self-raising flour

3 tablespoons polyunsaturated margarine

70 g dark muscovado sugar

80 g jumbo oats

¼ teaspoon freshly grated nutmeg

caster sugar, for sprinkling

4 ramekins, 200 ml each

Serves 4

Preparation time: 10 minutes

Put the plums, water and sugar in a saucepan. Heat until simmering, then simmer for 10–15 minutes, until the plums are just cooked and soft.

Meanwhile, to make the crumble topping, put the flour in a mixing bowl, add the margarine and rub it in with the tips of your fingers. The mixture should resemble breadcrumbs. Add the sugar, oats and nutmeg and mix.

Divide the plums and their cooking liquid between the 4 ramekins. Top with the crumble mixture, then sprinkle with a little caster sugar.

Bake in a preheated oven at 180°C (350°F) Gas 4 for 15–20 minutes, until the topping is golden and the fruit is bubbling. Serve warm with some half-fat crème fraîche, low-fat custard or ice cream.

Variation: Replace the plums with apples, cherries, pears, apricots, peaches or mixed berries. For some extra spice, add 1 tablespoon of grated fresh ginger to the crumble mixture.

NUTRITIONAL INFORMATION
Kcal: **473**
Fat: **12 g (3 g saturated)**
Protein: **8 g**
Carbohydrate: **72 g**

pan-cooked apples in red wine

This is a really wholesome, comforting pudding and yet it is still low in calories and saturated fat. It's particularly good eaten on a cold winter's evening with some low-fat custard.

4 eating apples, peeled, cored and cut into thick wedges

2 tablespoons freshly squeezed lemon juice

40 g polyunsaturated margarine

60 g light muscovado sugar

a few strips of unwaxed orange zest

freshly squeezed juice of 1 small orange

1 cinnamon stick, broken

150 ml red wine

225 g raspberries, thawed if frozen

150 ml low-fat vanilla ice cream, to serve

Serves 4

Preparation time: 10 minutes

Put the apple wedges in a bowl, sprinkle the lemon juice over the top and toss to coat. Heat a non-stick frying pan, add the margarine and melt gently over low heat. Add the sugar and stir to form a paste. Add the apple wedges to the pan and cook for 2 minutes, turning the apple over after 1 minute so it is well coated with the sugar paste.

Add the orange zest and juice, cinnamon pieces and wine to the pan. Bring to the boil, then reduce the heat and simmer gently for 12 minutes, stirring occasionally. Add the raspberries to the pan and cook for a further 1–2 minutes, until the apples are tender. Discard the orange zest and cinnamon pieces.

Transfer the apple and raspberry mixture to a serving plate and serve with 1 tablespoon of low-fat vanilla ice cream.

Variation: For an extra special dessert, add 2 tablespoons of Calvados to the red wine.

NUTRITIONAL INFORMATION
Kcal: **253**
Fat: **6 g (2 g saturated)**
Protein: **3 g**
Carbohydrate: **41 g**

baked apples with blackberries and port sauce

4 cooking apples, rinsed and cored

1 tablespoon freshly squeezed lemon juice

50 g blackberries, thawed if frozen

1 tablespoon flaked almonds

½ teaspoon ground allspice

½ teaspoon finely grated unwaxed lemon zest

300 ml ruby port

4 tablespoons clear honey

1 cinnamon stick, bruised

2 teaspoons cornflour

To serve (optional)

low-fat custard

lemon balm sprigs

a shallow ovenproof dish

Serves 4

Not only are apples low on the glycaemic index (38) but they are high in fibre. One large unpeeled apple contains 6 grams of fibre, which is approximately one quarter of the daily amount our bodies need for good health. If blackberries are not available, use blueberries instead.

Preparation time: 10 minutes

Make a shallow cut through the skin around the middle of each apple with a small, sharp knife – this will help the apples to cook. Brush the centres of the cored apples with the lemon juice to prevent them browning and stand them in a shallow ovenproof dish.

Put the blackberries, almonds, allspice and lemon zest in a bowl and mix. Using a teaspoon, spoon the mixture into the centre of each apple. Pour the port into the dish around the apples, and drizzle the honey over the fruit. Add the cinnamon stick to the dish and bake in a preheated oven at 200°C (400°F) Gas 6 for 35–40 minutes, until the apples are soft and tender.

Transfer the apples to a plate and keep warm in a low oven. Discard the cinnamon stick, then pour the cooking juices into a saucepan. Bring to the boil. Put the cornflour in a small bowl and blend to a smooth paste with 1 tablespoon of water. Add the paste to the boiling liquid and cook, stirring, until thickened.

Transfer the apples to a serving plate and pour over the port sauce. Serve immediately with some low-fat custard and a few lemon balm sprigs, if using.

NUTRITIONAL INFORMATION
Kcal: 279
Fat: 3 g (0 g saturated)
Protein: 3 g
Carbohydrate: 45 g

poached peaches in lemongrass syrup

Peaches have a GI rating of about 38 so they make a perfect basis for a pudding. This combination of white wine, sugar, ginger and lemongrass is really light and refreshing and packed full of taste.

400 ml dry white wine

400 ml water

1 stalk lemongrass, thinly sliced

2 cm piece fresh ginger, thinly sliced

1 bay leaf

100 g demerara sugar

4 large peaches, about 150 g each, halved and stoned

4 tablespoons low-fat yoghurt or half-fat crème fraîche, to serve

Serves 4

Preparation time: 5 minutes

Put the wine, water, lemongrass, ginger, bay leaf and sugar in a large non-stick frying pan and heat gently over low heat. Simmer for 5 minutes. Add the peach halves and poach for 5 minutes. Remove the peaches from the pan with a slotted spoon and set aside. When cool enough to handle, peel off the skins.

Bring the syrup to the boil and simmer for 10 minutes, until the syrup has reduced by half. Remove the pan from the heat and strain the syrup into a jug.

To serve, drizzle the syrup over the peaches and accompany with some low-fat yoghurt or half-fat crème fraîche.

Variation: Nectarines, plums or apricots would work equally well in this recipe. Omit the lemongrass and add 2 whole star anise, 4–5 cracked green cardamom pods and a twist of unwaxed lime zest for an aromatic syrup.

NUTRITIONAL INFORMATION
Kcal: **214**
Fat: **0 g**
Protein: **5 g**
Carbohydrate: **39 g**

hot jamaican chocolate bananas

These are a favourite with adults and children, just leave out the rum if you are serving these to kids. They are really easy to make and can be cooked on the barbecue, too, so they make a great sweet treat for both winter and summer. Chocolate has a GI rating of about 49, which makes it a fairly low-GI food. However, its high fat content means that it should still be eaten in small quantities. If you're a chocolate fan, melt a small amount and add to milk to make a sauce for desserts that has all the taste without all the calories.

4 firm bananas

50 ml rum (optional)

100 g plain chocolate, grated

100 g low-fat vanilla ice cream
or frozen yoghurt

16 fresh raspberries, to serve

a baking sheet

Serves 4

Preparation time: 5 minutes

NUTRITIONAL INFORMATION
Kcal: **350**
Fat: **9 g (4 g saturated)**
Protein: **4 g**
Carbohydrate: **49 g**

Put each banana on a square of foil. Pour over the rum, if using, and wrap up to make a parcel. Put the parcels on a baking sheet and bake in the centre of a preheated oven at 190°C (375°F) Gas 5 for 5 minutes.

Put the chocolate in a small bowl and melt in a microwave oven on high for 4 minutes, stirring halfway through. Alternatively, put the chocolate in a bowl and melt gently over a pan of simmering water.

Remove the bananas from the oven, carefully unwrap the foil parcels and transfer the bananas to a serving plate or bowl. Add 4 raspberries to each plate, then drizzle with the melted chocolate. Serve immediately with a scoop of ice cream or frozen yoghurt.

Variation: Make a quick Knickerbocker Glory by layering the warm bananas, scoops of low-fat ice cream and raspberries. Meanwhile, melt the chocolate with the rum, stir until smooth, then pour over the bananas and ice cream. Sprinkle the top with a few toasted flaked almonds, if you like.

cheat's cherry brûlée

The traditional recipe for crème brûlée uses cream and eggs, which would push the fat content sky-high. I love this alternative because it still tastes great but contains a lot less fat. Cherries are one of the lowest-GI foods available, too, so this brûlée really does have it all.

Preparation time: 15 minutes

Put the cherries in a saucepan with 100 ml water. Cook over high heat until simmering, then lower the heat and let simmer gently until the fruit is slightly softened, 5–7 minutes. Remove the pan from the heat.

Put the cream or crème fraîche, fromage frais and vanilla extract in a bowl and mix well. Divide the cherries between the 4 ramekins. Spoon the cream mixture over the cherries, then top each serving with 1 tablespoon of demerara sugar.

Put the ramekins under a preheated hot grill until the sugar melts and begins to caramelize. Remove from the heat and serve immediately.

Variation: If you are making this dessert for a special occasion, soak the cherries in 2–3 tablespoons of kirsch liqueur or cherry brandy before topping with the cream mixture. (This will add 64 kcals to each serving). If you prefer a cold pudding, put the brûlées in the refrigerator to chill. This will make the sugar set, making it even crunchier. If you prefer, replace the cherries with plums, which also have a low-GI rating.

300 g fresh, ripe cherries, stoned

100 ml half-fat cream or half-fat crème fraîche

100 ml low-fat fromage frais

1 teaspoon vanilla extract

4 tablespoons demerara sugar

4 ramekins, 150 ml each

Serves 4

NUTRITIONAL INFORMATION
Kcal: **165**
Fat: **3 g (1 g saturated)**
Protein: **3 g**
Carbohydrate: **30 g**

ginger rhubarb and lemon cream cups

The bite of the ginger and rhubarb against the mellowness of the cream makes this dessert irresistible. It is just as good served straight from a large bowl for a mid-week treat or in tall glasses for a dinner party.

2–3 tablespoons clear honey

1–2 teaspoons ground ginger

200 ml water

400 g rhubarb, trimmed and chopped into 5 cm pieces

200 ml low-fat fromage frais or half-fat crème fraîche

25 g icing sugar

1 tablespoon finely grated unwaxed lemon zest, plus extra strips, to serve

4 tall glasses

Serves 4

Preparation time: 10–12 minutes

Put the honey, ground ginger and water in a frying pan. Heat gently over medium heat and slowly bring to the boil, stirring occasionally. Reduce the heat and simmer for 10 minutes. Add the rhubarb to the pan and simmer for a further 8 minutes, until the rhubarb is soft but still holding its shape. Remove the pan from the heat and let cool.

Drain the rhubarb, then divide it between 4 tall glasses. Chill in the refrigerator for 1 hour. Just before serving, put the fromage frais or crème fraîche, icing sugar and lemon zest in a bowl and mix. Spoon the mixture on top of the rhubarb and serve sprinkled with strips of lemon zest.

Variation: Make an instant fool by combining the cooked rhubarb and the crème fraîche or fromage frais. Spoon into individual dishes, chill, then serve sprinkled with strips of lemon zest.

NUTRITIONAL INFORMATION
Kcal: **166**
Fat: **6 g (3 g saturated)**
Protein: **2 g**
Carbohydrate: **26 g**

orange and mango 'ice cream'

I love this dessert, as does my two-year-old boy. The mango blends with the yoghurt and crème fraîche in such a way as to make this pudding taste deliciously creamy, just like ice cream. It is a fantastic cheat of a recipe because although it is extremely quick and easy to make, a great way of 'upping' your fruit intake, packed full of the immune-boosting vitamins A and C and very low in fat, it tastes rich, creamy and decidedly wicked!

Preparation time: 15 minutes

Set your freezer to rapid freeze at least 30 minutes before required and remember to return it to its normal setting afterwards.

Scoop out the flesh from the oranges, leaving the skins intact. If necessary, cut a small slice off the base of each orange half so that they stand upright. Put the orange and mango flesh, orange zest, yoghurt and crème fraîche in a blender. Blend for a few minutes until smooth. Spoon the mixture into a freezeable container and freeze for 2 hours, stirring occasionally to break up the ice crystals.

Spoon the mixture into the orange halves. Return to the freezer and leave for at least 1 hour, or until frozen solid. Let soften in the refrigerator for at least 30 minutes before serving. Serve 2 orange halves per person sprinkled with some freshly grated chocolate.

Variation: You could use pink grapefruit instead of the oranges; add 2 tablespoons of finely grated zest to the yoghurt mixture. You could simply freeze the mixture in a container and serve it in scoops after letting it soften in the refrigerator.

4 large oranges, halved

2 large mangoes, peeled and stoned

2 tablespoons finely grated unwaxed orange zest

3 tablespoons low-fat natural yoghurt

3 tablespoons low-fat crème fraîche

2 squares plain chocolate, grated

Serves 4

NUTRITIONAL INFORMATION
Kcal: 191
Fat: 4 g (1.5 g saturated)
Protein: 4 g
Carbohydrate: 38 g

Index

FEEDBACK

I genuinely enjoy eating a low-GI Diet and most people I speak to that make the switch do, too. It's healthy, tasty, easy to do and can easily be adopted as a lifelong eating strategy rather than just a quick fix diet. The really great thing about it is that although it results in a loss of excess pounds it is so much more than just a weight-loss diet because eating this way naturally increases your energy levels and reduces your chances of suffering from the three biggest killers, heart disease, cancer and diabetes.

I'm really interested to hear any feedback you may have about the ideas and recipes in this book, in particular your personal experiences with adopting a low-GI way of eating so please do e-mail any comments you might have to
high.energy@ntlworld.com

ACKNOWLEDGMENTS

I'd like to thank:

Joanna McMillan, Rick Mendosa, Duane Mellor and Jennie Brand Miller for taking the time out of their very busy lives to answer my queries and provide invaluable feedback and support.

Gina Steer for her tireless pursuit of perfection, Sharon Ashman for her attention to detail and Alison Starling for being open to new ideas and allowing me the opportunity to express them in the form of this book.

Hannah Miller for her unnatural ability to decipher my scribblings plus her boundless enthusiasm for all things foody and last but not least, Samantha Murphy for helping to make it all happen in the first place!

On a personal note I'd also like to thank:

Louis James, for all his wise words not to mention his endless encouragement, love, support, kindness – and patience.

Jill Barr for keeping all the plates spinning, Lou Holt for enabling her to do so and last, but by no means least, my two beautiful little boys for being ... just that.